1,001

Liverpool F.C

Quiz Questions

Plus Statistics, History & Fun Facts

1,001

Liverpool F.C

Quiz Questions

MARTIN FLANNAGAN

Table of Contents

HOW DID YOU DO?

The Early Years

1. When was Liverpool Football Club formed?
(a) 15 March 1892   (b) 15 November 1892   (c) 15 March 1893

2. Who was the founder?
(a) Robert Houlding   (b) John Houlding   (c) Theodore Houlding

3. What did he also found?
(a) Littlewoods   (b) Liverpool Cricket Club   (c) Anfield Masonic Lodge

4. What was his profession?
(a) brewer   (b) foundry owner   (c) ship owner

5. What political office did he attain in 1897?
(a) Lord Mayor of Liverpool   (b) MP for Liverpool East
(c) Sheriff of Liverpool

6. What were the club's first colours?
(a) black and white   (b) blue and white   (c) green and white

7. When did the club start wearing red shirts?
(a) 1894   (b) 1896   (c) 1898

8. Which League did they first join?
(a) Liverpool & District League   (b) Football Alliance
(c) Lancashire League

9. Who was the club's first manager?
(a) Robert McNamara   (b) John McDonald   (c) John McKenna

10. What was his team nicknamed owing to the number of Scottish players?
(a) The Clanfields   (b) The Scots Terriers   (c) The team of Macs

11. What cup competition did they win in their first season?
(a) Lancashire Senior Cup   (b) Liverpool District Cup
(c) Lancashire Junior Cup

12. When did the club join the Football League?
(a) 1893   (b) 1895   (c) 1897

13. Who were the first League opponents?
(a) Woolwich Arsenal   (b) Middlesbrough Ironopolis
(c) Sheffield United

14. What position did Liverpool finish in the first season in the Second Division?
(a) first   (b) fourth   (c) seventh

15. Who was appointed manager in 1896?
(a) Tom Watson   (b) David Blunkett   (c) Jack Straw

16. What was his annual salary?
(a) £100   (b) £300   (c) £900

17. In which season did Liverpool first reach an FA Cup semi-final?
(a) 1894-95   (b) 1896–97   (c) 1898-99

18. In which season did they win their first League title?
(a) 1900-01   (b) 1903-04   (c) 1906-07

19. Who was the leading goalscorer that season, who went on to score 127 goals in 224 games for the club?
(a) Ray Boulder   (b) Gordon Hodgson   (c) Sam Raybould

20. Who was the captain, who played 341 games for the club from 1898 to 1909?
(a) Don Mackinlay   (b) Alex Raisbeck   (c) Ephraim Longworth

(Answers p153)

Liverpool Facts

Kenny Dalglish was the first ever player-manager in professional English football. During his five years in charge Liverpool won three League titles and two FA Cups.

In the 1984-85 season, John Wark became the first Liverpool player to score a hat-trick in three different competitions: the European Cup, the FA Cup and the League. So far, he is the only player to do it.

Jamie Carragher

1. In which Merseyside town was Jamie Carragher born ?
(a) Birkenhead   (b) Bootle   (c) St Helens

2. Which team did he support growing up?
(a) Liverpool   (b) Tranmere   (c) Everton

3. In what season did he make his full Liverpool debut?
(a) 1995-96   (b) 1996-97   (c) 1997-98

4. What was his squad number at Liverpool from 1996 to his retirement?
(a) 5   (b) 17   (c) 23

5. Which tournament did he miss because of knee surgery?
(a) 2002 World Cup   (b) 2004 European Championships
(c) 2006 World Cup

6. How many seasons did he spend in the Liverpool first team?
(a) 16   (b) 17   (c) 18

7. How many appearances did he make for Liverpool?
(a) 537   (b) 637   (c) 737

8. Which teammate did he clash with during the game vs West Brom in May 2009?
(a) Daniel Agger   (b) Xabi Alonso   (c) Álvaro Arbeloa

9. How tall is he?
(a) 5ft 11   (b) 6ft 1   (c) 6ft 3

10. Who were the opponents in the April 2011 game in which Carragher was knocked out following a collision with teammate Jon Flanagan?
(a) Arsenal   (b) West Ham   (c) Chelsea

11. How many times was he voted Liverpool Player of the Season?
(a) one   (b) two   (c) three

12. How many goals did he score for Liverpool?
(a) 5   (b) 10   (c) 15

13. How much did he donate to his 23 Foundation charity when setting it up in 2009?
(a) £500,000   (b) £1million   (c) £2million

14. How many full England caps did he earn?
(a) 38   (b) 48   (c) 58

15. What is the title of his autobiography?
(a) 23 Red   (b) Simply Red: The Jamie Carragher Story
(c) Carra: My Autobiography

(Answers p154)

The 1976–77 European Cup

1. Which country were first round opponents Crusaders from?
(a) Malta   (b) Northern Ireland   (c) Eire

2. What was the first round aggregate score?
(a) 5-0   (b) 6-0   (c) 7-0

3. Who were the opponents in the second round?
(a) Trabzonspor   (b) Dynamo Kyiv   (c) Zurich

4. How long did it take to score the three goals in the 3-0 second leg win at Anfield?
(a) 12mins   (b) 19mins   (c) 26mins

5. Who were the quarter-final opponents?
(a) Dynamo Dresden (b) Club Brugge   (c) Saint-Etienne

6. Who scored the goal that put Liverpool through to the semi-final?
(a) Kevin Keegan   (b) David Fairclough   (c) Jimmy Case

7. How much time had been played when he scored?
(a) 84mins   (b) 87mins   (c) 90mins

8. Who scored twice in the first leg of the semi-final?
(a) Phil Neal   (b) Terry McDermott   (c) Ray Kennedy

9. What was the aggregate score in the semi-final?
(a) 4-1   (b) 5-2   (c) 6-1

10. In which stadium was the final staged?
(a) San Siro (b) Stadio Artemio Franchi (c) Stadio Olimpico

11. What was the attendance?
(a) 42,000 (b) 52,000 (c) 62,000

12. Who scored Liverpool's third goal in the final?
(a) Tommy Smith (b) Phil Neal (c) Kevin Keegan

(Answers p154)

How Tall?

The current squad

	Player	Height
1	Alisson	
2	Adrian	
3	Virgil van Dijk	
4	Joe Gomez	
5	Andy Robertson	
6	Joel Matip	
7	Trent Alexander-Arnold	
8	Fabinho	
9	Georginio Wijnaldum	
10	Thiago	
11	James Milner	
12	Naby Keita	
13	Jordan Henderson	
14	Alex Oxlade-Chamberlain	
15	Curtis Jones	
16	Diogo Jota	
17	Xherdan Shaqiri	
18	Roberto Firmino	
19	Sadio Mane	
20	Mohamed Salah	

Score half a point if you're an inch out either way. Half inches are rounded up.

The author accepts no responsibility for the use of platform shoes.

(Answers p155)

Anagrams

Rearrange the letters to form the names of famous Liverpool players. The years they were at the club are in brackets.

(1) Mainly dockland
(1910–1929)

_ _ _ _ _ _ / _ _ _ _ _ _ _ _

(2) Blacker jam
(1935–1952)

_ _ _ _ / _ _ _ _ _ _

(3) An oyster
(1961–1971)

_ _ _ / _ _ _ _ _

(4) Monet prophets
(1963–1973)

_ _ _ _ _ / _ _ _ _ _ _ _ _

(5) Rename cycle
(1967–1981)

_ _ _ / _ _ _ _ _ _ _ _

(6) Jock not shah
(1970–1978)

_ _ _ _ / _ _ _ _ _ _ _

(7) A hen pill
(1974–1985)

_ _ _ _ / _ _ _ _

(8) Lay memes
(1976–1986)

_ _ _ _ _ / _ _ _

(9) Nanny leaked   _ _ _ _ / _ _ _ _ _ _ _ _
    (1978–1986)

(10) Klansman rower   _ _ _ _ / _ _ _ _ _ _ _ _ _
    (1981–1988)

(Answers p155)

The Shoot-outs

1974 Charity Shield
Wembley, Sat 10 Aug
Liverpool 1 - 1 **Leeds United**

Line-up: Tommy Smith, Alec Lindsay, Phil Thompson, Peter Cormack, Emlyn Hughes (capt), Kevin Keegan, Brian Hall, Steve Heighway, Ian Callaghan, Phil Boersma

Fill in the names of Liverpool's penalty takers below

	Liverpool			Leeds	
			0 - 1	Peter Lorimer	scored
1		scored	1 - 1		
			1 - 2	Johnny Giles	scored
2		scored	2 - 2		
			2 - 3	Eddie Gray	scored
3		scored	3 - 3		
			3 - 4	Norman Hunter	scored
4		scored	4 - 4		
			4 - 5	Trevor Cherry	scored
5		scored	5 - 5		
			5 - 5	David Harvey	missed
6		scored	6 - 5		

(Answers p156)

Mohamed Salah

1. In what year was Mohamed Salah born?
(a) 1988   (b) 1990   (c) 1992

2. In what country was he born?
(a) Egypt   (b) Algeria   (c) Tunisia

3. How long did it take a 14-year-old Salah to travel to training each day?
(a) 2-2½ hrs   (b) 3-3½ hrs   (c) 4-4½ hrs

4. At which club did he begin his playing career?
(a) Aswan SC   (b) Al Mokawloon   (c) Al Masry

5. Which Swiss club did he join in 2012?
(a) Basel   (b) FC Zürich   (c) FC St. Gallen

6. Which Premier League club did he sign for in 2014?
(a) Tottenham   (b) West Ham   (c) Chelsea

7. Which Italian club did he sign for in August 2016?
(a) Roma   (b) Juventus   (c) Lazio

8. What was the fee?
(a) €5 million   (b) €15 million   (c) €25 million

9. When did he sign for Liverpool?
(a) Jun 2016   (b) Jan 2017   (c) Jun 2017

10. How much did Liverpool pay for him?
(a) £26.5m   (b) £36.5m   (c) £46.5m

11. How many games did it take him to score his first 20 goals for Liverpool?
(a) 26   (b) 30   (c) 34

12. How many did he score in the 5–0 win over Watford in March 2018?
(a) three   (b) four   (c) five

13. How many goals did he score in the 2018-19 season?
(a) 36   (b) 40   (c) 44

14. What nickname have Liverpool fans given him?
(a) Mighty Mo   (b) Super Sal   (c) Egyptian King

15. How many times has he won the Premier League Golden Boot?
(a) one   (b) two   (c) three

(Answers p156)

The 1977–78 European Cup

1. Who were Liverpool's second round opponents?
(a) Red Star Belgrade   (b) Levski-Spartak   (c) Dynamo
Dresden

2. What was the result in the first leg at Anfield?
(a) 3-1   (b) 5-1   (c) 7-1

3. Who were the quarter-final opponents?
(a) Benfica   (b) Atletico Madrid   (c) Ajax

4. Who scored the winning goal in the first leg?
(a) Phil Neal   (b) Jimmy Case   (c) Emlyn Hughes

5. Who were the semi-final opponents?
(a) Juventus   (b) Bayern Munich   (c) Borussia
Monchengladbach

**6. Who scored Liverpool's goal in the first leg of the
semi-final in Germany?**
(a) David Johnson   (b) Kenny Dalglish   (c) Ray Kennedy

7. Where did the game take place?
(a) Frankfurt   (b) Dortmund   (c) Dusseldorf

8. What was the aggregate score of the semi-final?
(a) 3-2   (b) 4-2   (c) 5-2

9. Who did Liverpool meet in the final?
(a) Club Brugge   (b) Lillestrom   (c) Malmo

10. Where was the final played?
(a) Hampden Park   (b) Parc des Princes   (c) Wembley
Stadium

11. Who scored the only goal of the game?
(a) Graeme Souness   (b) Kenny Dalglish   (c) Ray Kennedy

**12. Who was Liverpool's top scorer in the competition
that season?**
(a) Kenny Dalglish   (b) Phil Neal   (c) Jimmy Case

(Answers p157)

Liverpool Facts

Between 1973 and 1991, Liverpool finished outside of the
top two just once, when they finished fifth in 1981. They
did, however, win their third European Cup that season.

Liverpool were the first club to feature on BBC1's *Match of
the Day* in 1964. They also featured in the first-ever game
televised in colour in 1969.

Ian Rush

1. In what year was Ian Rush born?
(a) 1958   (b) 1961   (c) 1964

2. Which League club did he first play for?
(a) Wrexham   (b) Cardiff City   (c) Chester City

3. How old was he when he first signed for Liverpool?
(a) 18   (b) 19   (c) 20

4. What was the transfer fee?
(a) £100,000   (b) £200,000   (c) £300,000

5. How long did it take him to score on his debut?
(a) 3 minutes   (b) 13 minutes   (c) 33 minutes

6. Who were the opponents when he scored in the 1982 League Cup Final?
(a) West Ham   (b) Tottenham   (c) Chelsea

7. Which Italian club did he sign for in 1986?
(a) Inter Milan   (b) Roma   (c) Juventus

8. What was the transfer fee?
(a) £1.2m   (b) £2.2m   (c) £3.2m

9. How much did Liverpool pay to re-sign Rush in August 1988?
(a) £1.7m   (b) £2.7m   (c) £3.7m

10. How many goals did he score for Liverpool?
(a) 296   (b) 346   (c) 396

11. How many full Wales caps did he earn?
(a) 33   (b) 53   (c) 73

12. In how many seasons was he Liverpool's top goalscorer?
(a) six   (b) eight   (c) ten

13. What was the last British club he played for?
(a) Chester City   (b) Wrexham   (c) Leeds

14. What honour was he awarded in 1996?
(a) MBE   (b) OBE   (c) CBE

15. Which club did he manage from 2004 to 2005?
(a) Chester City   (b) Wrexham   (c) Leeds

(Answers p157)

Name the Three...

... Liverpool players in England's 1966 World Cup squad

1 _____

2 . _____

3. _____

... Most recent players to score on their first-team debut for Liverpool

1 _____ (Jan 2013 v Mansfield)

2 _____ (Sep 2012 v Young Boys)

3 _____ (Feb 2011 v Stoke)

... Most recent players to score on their Premier League debut for Liverpool

1 _____ (Aug 2017 v Watford)

2 _____ (Aug 2016 v Arsenal)

3 _____ (Sep 2013 v Swansea)

... Seasons Liverpool won the Uefa Cup

1 _____

2 _____

3 _____

(Answers p158)

Liverpool Facts

Xavi Alonso held the record for longest Premier League goal by an outfield player (63 yards against Newcastle) until former Liverpool player Charlie Adam scored from 66 yards.

After signing for Liverpool Danish keeper Michael Stensgaard dislocated his shoulder setting up an ironing board and was never able to play a game for the club.

Transfers: The 1960s

Match the following clubs to the Liverpool signings

Arsenal   Dundee United
Blackpool   Motherwell
Bristol Rovers   Preston
Burnley   Scunthorpe
Bury   Wolves

	Date	Player	Fee	Signed from
1	Aug 1960	Gordon Milne	£16,000	
2	May 1961	Ian St John	£37,500	
3	Jul 1961	Ron Yeats	£22,000	
4	Feb 1962	Jim Furnell	£18,000	
5	Nov 1964	Geoff Strong	£40,000	
6	Feb 1967	Emlyn Hughes	£65,000	
7	Jun 1967	Ray Clemence	£18,000	
8	Sep 1968	Alun Evans	£100,000	
9	Mar 1969	Alec Lindsay	£67,000	
10	Apr 1969	Larry Lloyd	£50,000	

(Answers p158)

Who Said That?

1. "Liverpool Football Club exists to win trophies."
(a) Bob Paisley   (b) Bill Shankly   (c) Rafa Benitez

2. "Liverpool players must play like a lion, give his all. There must be determination, commitment and resolve to be a Liverpool player."
(a) Kevin Keegan   (b) Jurgen Klopp   (c) Gerard Houllier

3. "If you're in the penalty area and don't know what to do with the ball, put it in the net and we'll discuss the options later."
(a) Bob Paisley   (b) Bill Shankly   (c) Roy Evans

4. "Before, I said that they were maybe the best supporters in England. Now maybe they are the best supporters in Europe."
(a) Emlyn Hughes   (b) Rafa Benitez   (c) Bob Paisley

5. "For a player to be good enough to play for Liverpool, he must be prepared to run through a brick wall for me then come out fighting on the other side."
(a) Graeme Souness   (b) Bill Shankly   (c) Gerard Houllier

6. "Put 'WE LIED' on the front page of your newspaper."
(a) Alan Hansen   (b) Graeme Souness   (c) Kenny Dalglish

7. "Steve Nicol never gives more than 120 per cent."
(a) Joe Fagan   (b) Graeme Souness   (c) Kevin Keegan

8. "When I die, don't bring me to the hospital. Bring me to Anfield. I was born there and will die there."
(a) Steven Gerrard   (b) Bill Shankly   (c) Jamie Carragher

9. "Sometimes I feel I'm hardly wanted in this Liverpool team. If I get two or three saves to make I've had a busy day."
(a) Bruce Grobbelaar   (b) Ray Clemence   (c) Pepe Reina

10. "If Everton were playing at the bottom of my garden, I'd shut the curtains."
(a) Bill Shankly   (b) Emlyn Hughes   (c) Kenny Dalglish

(Answers p159)

Name the Season

1. Liverpool lose 1-0 at Sunderland after a Darren Bent shot deflects off a beach ball that had been thrown onto the field by a spectator. Rafael Benítez leaves the club at the end of the season after a seventh place finish in the Premier League.

2. John Aldridge is signed from Oxford in January for £750,000. Sammy Lee is sold to QPR. Liverpool lose to Arsenal in the League Cup final.

3. Phil Thompson makes his debut in a 3-0 win at Old Trafford on Easter Monday. Liverpool finish third in the League, one point behind the champions.

4. John Aldridge leaves for Spain. Liverpool beat Crystal Palace 1-0 then lose 4-3 to them in the FA Cup semi-final.

5. Jordan Henderson becomes club captain. A shock announcement is made after eight games. Liverpool finish trophy-less despite reaching two finals.

6. Rob Jones signs from Crewe for £300,000. Liverpool lose 1–0 to Third Division Peterborough in the fourth round of the League Cup. John Beresford misses a penalty for Portsmouth to send Liverpool to Wembley.

7. Stan Collymore signs in the close season for a British record fee of £8.5million. Liverpool beat Rochdale 7-0 in the third round of the FA Cup.

8. Assistant manager Phil Thompson takes charge after Gerard Houllier is forced to take a five-month break because of a heart condition. Liverpool finish second, seven points behind Arsenal.

9. Bruce Grobbelaar, Mark Lawrenson and Ian Rush make their debuts. Liverpool are knocked out the European Cup by CSKA Sofia.

10. Liverpool record the biggest away win by an English side in European competition with a 7-0 victory at Maribor. A major departure and new signing occur in January. Salah's season ends with a dislocated shoulder.

11. Graeme Souness signs from Middlesbrough for £352,000. Liverpool beat Kevin Keegan's Hamburg 6-0 to win the Super Cup.

(Answers p159)

Where are they from?
The current squad

Fill in the players' countries of birth below

	Player	Apps	Goals	Country of birth
1	Alisson	112	0	
2	Adrian	23	0	
3	Virgil van Dijk	130	13	
4	Joel Matip	123	6	
5	Fabinho	107	3	
6	Georginio Wijnaldum	218	22	
7	Thiago	12	0	
8	Naby Keita	71	7	
9	Xherdan Shaqiri	55	8	
10	Roberto Firmino	276	84	
11	Sadio Mane	199	91	
12	Mohamed Salah	184	116	
13	Diogo Jota	17	9	
14	Divock Origi	155	35	

Figures correct to end of 2019-20 season

(Answers p160)

Kevin Keegan

1. Where was Kevin Keegan born?
(a) Hull   (b) Rotherham   (c) Doncaster

2. Where did Keegan work as an office clerk after leaving school aged 15?
(a) a brass works   (b) an accountants   (c) a coal mine

3. Which club did he first play for?
(a) Scunthorpe   (b) Hull   (c) Blyth Spartans

4. What was the transfer fee when he joined Liverpool in 1971?
(a) £13,000   (b) £33,000   (c) £66,000

5. What was his initial wage after signing?
(a) £50 a week   (b) £150 a week   (c) £300 a week

6. How many appearances did he make for Liverpool?
(a) 232   (b) 323   (c) 423

7. How many goals did he score for Liverpool?
(a) 100   (b) 150   (c) 200

8. Who famously punched Keegan in the 1974 Charity Shield?
(a) Billy Bremner   (b) Norman Hunter   (c) Johnny Giles

9. How did he get injured competing in BBC TV's _Superstars_ in 1976?
(a) he tripped over a hurdle   (b) he crashed his bicycle
(c) he capsized his canoe

10. How many full England caps did he earn?
(a) 63   (b) 83   (c) 103

11. Which German club did join in 1977?
(a) Bayern Munich   (b) Borussia Mönchengladbach
(c) Hamburg

12. What was the transfer fee?
(a) £300,000   (b) £500,000   (c) £700,000

13. What was the name of his song that reached number 31 in the UK Singles Chart in 1979?
(a) Head Over Heels in Love   (b) Football Crazy
(c) Anarchy in the UK

14. Which English club did he join after returning from Germany in 1980?
(a) Brighton   (b) Newcastle   (c) Southampton

15. Which brand of aftershave did he advertise in the 1980s?
(a) Lynx   (b) Brut   (c) Old Spice

(Answers p160)

Shoot-outs 2

1984 European Cup Final
Stadio Olimpico, Wed 30 May
Liverpool 1 - 1 **Roma**

Lineup: Phil Neal, Mark Lawrenson, Alan Hansen, Alan Kennedy, Craig Johnston, Sammy Lee, Graeme Souness (capt), Ronnie Whelan, Kenny Dalglish, Ian Rush
Subs: Michael Robinson, Steve Nicol

Fill in in the names of Liverpool's penalty takers below

	Liverpool			Roma	
1		missed	0 - 0		
			0 - 1	A. Di Bartolomei	scored
2		scored	1 - 1		
			1 - 1	Bruno Conti	missed
3		scored	2 - 1		
			2 - 2	Urbaldo Righetti	scored
4		scored	3 - 2		
			3 - 2	Francesco Graziani	missed
5		scored	4 - 2		

(Answers p161)

Who am I?

1. I was born in Llandudno and joined Liverpool from Wrexham. I score three goals in 100 appearances for the club and won two European Cups. It is said I eat frogs legs.

2. I played 650 games for Liverpool before ending my playing days at Bolton, one of four clubs I managed. I played in the 1982 World Cup finals and later became England's assistant manager.

3. Born in Kirkby, I used to stand on the Kop as a boy. I've won three European Cups and captained England six times. After ending my playing career at Sheffield United I returned to the club.

4. I played for Liverpool for 19 seasons. I played for England in the 1966 World Cup but did not win a medal. In my 979-game career I was only booked once.

5. I was born in Dublin and have a degree in economics and politics. After ending my playing days in the United States I took charge of a famous academy.

6. Born in Liverpool in 1957, I made nine substitute appearances in my first season. I was also the substitute in Liverpool's first European Cup win.

7. Born in Cardiff, I joined Liverpool for a club record fee. I've managed 12 clubs on three continents and two national sides.

8. Born in Merseyside, I've played for both Liverpool clubs. After winning three League titles with Liverpool I moved to Manchester City, where I didn't win anything.

9. I was Bob Paisley's last signing when I joined from Shamrock Rovers. My first goal for the club was in a European Cup semi-final. Two bad injuries cut my Liverpool career short, and I retired from playing aged 27.

10. I signed for Liverpool four years after losing to them in an FA Cup final. I scored the only goal in one final for Liverpool and the all-important penalty in another.

(Answers p161)

Sadio Mane

1. In what year was Sadio Mane born?
(a) 1988   (b) 1990   (c) 1992

2. In which country was he born?
(a) Senegal   (b) Cameroon   (c) Ivory Coast

3. What was his first club?
(a) Lens   (b) Lyon   (c) Metz

4. Which Austrian club did he sign for in 2012?
(a) Sturm Graz   (b) Red Bull Salzburg   (c) Austria Wien

5. Which Premier League club did he join in September 2014?
(a) Brighton   (b) West Ham   (c) Southampton

6. What was the fee?
(a) £6.8 million   (b) £11.8 million   (c) £16.8 million

7. Sane holds the record for the fastest hat-trick in the Premier League. How long did he take?
(a) 2 mins 56 sec   (b) 3 mins 56 sec   (c) 4 mins 56 sec

8. When did he sign for Liverpool?
(a) Jan 2016   (b) Jun 2016   (c) Sep 2016

9. How much did Liverpool pay for him?
(a) £24 million   (b) £29 million   (c) £34 million

10 What award did he win in May 2017?
(a) Liverpool Player of the Season (b) PFA Player of the Season (c) Golden Boot:

11. At which ground did he receive a straight red card in Sept 2017?
(a) Stamford Bridge   (b) Emirates Stadium   (c) Ethiad Stadium

12. Who were the opponents when he scored his first Liverpool hat-trick in Feb 2018?
(a) Porto   (b) Lyon   (c) Benfica

13. How many goals did he score in the 2017-18 Champions League campaign?
(a) 6   (b) 8   (c) 10

14. How many goals did he score to become joint-winner of the Premier League Golden Boot in 2018–19?
(a) 20   (b) 22   (c) 24

15. How many Premier League games did he play that season?
(a) 30   (b) 33   (c) 36

(Answers p161)

Club Records

1. What is our record win?
(a) 9-0   (b) 11–0   (c) 13-1

2. What is the record league win?
(a) 10–1   (b) 9-1   (c) 8-0

3. What is the record defeat?
(a) 10-2   (b) 9-1   (c) 8-0

4. What is the highest number of league wins in a season?
(a) 26   (b) 29   (c) 32

5. What is the highest attendance for a Liverpool game?
(a) 94,827   (b) 101,254   (c) 112,803

6. What is the lowest number of league goals we've conceded in a season?
(a) 14   (b) 16   (c) 18

7. What is the record for consecutive league wins?
(a) 18   (b) 16   (c) 14

8. What is the record FA Cup win?
(a) 9–0   (b) 8-0   (c) 7-0

9. What are the most goals scored in a top flight season?
(a) 97   (b) 101   (c) 105

10. What is the highest number of consecutive home matches without defeat?
(a) 65   (b) 75   (c) 85

(Answers p162)

Anfield

1. In which country is the town of Annefield, after which Anfield is named?
(a) Scotland (b) Ireland (c) Wales

2. When was Anfield opened?
(a) 1884 (b) 1888 (c) 1892

3. What was the attendance for Liverpool's first League match there in 1893?
(a) 5,000 (b) 10,000 (c) 15,000

4. Which architect designed the stand that was built in 1895 on the site of the present Main Stand?
(a) Charles Barry (b) Archibald Leitch (c) Sir Christopher Wren

5. What is Anfield's record attendance?
(a) 57,905 (b) 61,905 (c) 65,905

6. What is the current capacity?
(a) 52,394 (b) 53,394 (c) 54,394

7. What will be the capacity after the planned Anfield Road Stand expansion?
(a) 59,000 (b) 60,000 (c) 61,000

8. When was the Spion Kop built?
(a) 1900 (b) 1906 (c) 1912

9. What was the Kop named after?
(a) a mountain in Scotland (b) a valley in Germany (c) a hill in South Africa

10. What was the Kop's capacity after it was redesigned in 1928?
(a) 20,000   (b) 25,000   (c) 30,000

11. Which manager introduced the 'THIS IS ANFIELD' sign?
(a) Phil Taylor   (b) Bill Shankly   (c) Bob Paisley

12. The topmast of which ship serves as a flagpole beside the entrance to the Kop?
(a) SS Great Eastern   (b) SS Great Britain
(c) SS Liverpool

13. In what year were floodlights installed?
(a) 1951   (b) 1954   (c) 1957

14. What was added in 1982?
(a) a club shop   (b) the Shankly Gates   (c) new floodlights

15. When was the Kemlyn Road stand renamed the Centenary Stand after a second tier was added?
(a) 1990   (b) 1992   (c) 1994

(Answers p162)

Michael Owen

1. Where was Michael Owen born?
(a) Chester   (b) Southport   (c) Liverpool

2. In what sport was his father, Terry, a professional?
(a) boxing   (b) rugby league   (c) football

3. In which season did he make his full Liverpool debut?
(a) 1994-95   (b) 1995-96   (c) 1996-97

4. How old was he on his full Liverpool debut?
(a) 16 yrs 11mths   (b) 17 yrs 4mths   (c) 17 yrs 9mths

5. How much did Real Madrid pay for him in the summer of 2004?
(a) £8 million   (b) £12 million   (c) £16 million

6. In what year did he win the Ballon d'Or?
(a) 1998   (b) 2001   (c) 2004

7. How many times did he win the Premier League Golden Boot?
(a) one   (b) two   (c) three

8. How many goals did he score for England in full internationals?
(a) 40   (b) 60   (c) 80

9. Against which country did he score a goal voted as the third-greatest in England's history?
(a) Spain   (b) Germany   (c) Argentina

10. In what year was he voted BBC Sports Personality of the Year?
(a) 1998   (b) 2001   (c) 2004

11. How many goals did he score for Liverpool?
(a) 158   (b) 178   (c) 198

12. How many full England caps did he earn?
(a) 69   (b) 89   (c) 109

13. Which brand of washing powder did he advertise from 2004?
(a) Ariel   (b) Persil   (c) Daz

14. Which English club did he join from Real Madrid in 2005?
(a) Man United   (b) Man City   (c) Newcastle

15. At which club did he finish his footballing career?
(a) Leicester   (b) Stoke   (c) Blackburn

(Answers p163)

Name the Five Players...

... Who have worn Liverpool's number five shirt in the Premier League

1 _____ (1993-98)

2 _____ (1998-00)

3 _____ (2001-05)

4 _____ (2005-14)

5 _____ (2016-20).

... Who have won the most England Caps while with Liverpool?

1 _____ (114)

2 _____ (60)

3 _____ (59)

4 _____ (56)

5 _____ (54).

... Who have scored the most goals for England with Liverpool?

1 _____ (26)

2 _____ (21)

3 _____ (18)

4 _____ (13)

5 _____ (8)

... Who have appeared for both Liverpool & Everton in the Premier League?

1 _____

2 _____

3 _____

4 _____

5 _____ .

… Who have captained European Cup / Champions League-winning teams

1 _____ (1977 & 1978)

2 _____ (1981)

3 _____ (1984)

4 _____ (2005)

5 _____ (2019).

… To score UEFA Champions League hat-tricks with Liverpool

1. _____ (3-1 v Spartak Moscow)

2. _____ (8-0 v Besiktaş, Nov 2007)

3. _____ (7-0 v Sp.Moscow, Dec 2017)

4. _____ (5-0 v Porto, Feb 2018)

5. _____ (5-0 v Atalanta, Nov 2020)

(Answers p164)

How Tall? (part 2)

	Player	Years at club	Height
1	Ian Callaghan	1959–1978	
2	Chris Lawler	1960–1975	
3	Ian St John	1961–1971	
4	Ron Yeats	1961–1971	
5	Tommy Smith	1962–1978	
6	Roger Hunt	1962–1969	
7	Ray Clemence	1967–1981	
8	Emlyn Hughes	1967–1979	
9	Steve Heighway	1970–1981	
10	John Toshack	1970–1978	
11	Phil Thompson	1971–1984	
12	Kevin Keegan	1971–1977	
13	Jimmy Case	1973–1981	
14	Terry McDermott	1974–1982	
15	Ray Kennedy	1974–1982	
16	Phil Neal	1974–1985	
17	Joey Jones	1975–1978	
18	David Fairclough	1975–1983	
19	Sammy Lee	1976–1986	
20	Kenny Dalglish	1977–1990	

Score half a point if you're an inch out either way. Half inches are rounded up.

(Answers p165)

Shoot-outs 3

2001 League Cup Final
Millennium Stadium, Sun 25 Feb
Liverpool 1 - 1 **Birmingham City**

Line-up: Sander Westerveld, Markus Babbel, Stephane Henchoz, Sami Hyypia, Jamie Carragher, Steven Gerrard, Dietmar Hamann, Igor Biscan, Vladimír Smicer, Emile Heskey, Robbie Fowler (capt)
Subs: Christian Ziege, Nick Barmby, Gary McAllister

Fill in in the names of Liverpool's penalty takers below

	Liverpool			Birmingham	
1		Scored	1 - 0		
			1 - 0	Martin Grainger	saved
2		Scored	2 - 0		
			2 - 1	Darren Purse	scored
3		Scored	3 - 1		
			3 - 2	Marcelo	scored
4		Saved	3 - 2		
			3 - 3	Stan Lazaridis	scored
5		Scored	4 - 3		
			4 - 4	Michael Hughes	scored
6		Scored	5 - 4		
			5 - 4	Andy Johnson	saved

(Answers p166)

The 1980–81 European Cup

1. What was the score in the first round second leg match vs Finnish side OPS?
(a) 6-1   (b) 8-1   (c) 10-1

2. Which two players scored hat-tricks in that game?
(a) Dalglish & Fairclough   (b) Souness & McDermott
(c) Neal & Lee

3. Who were Liverpool's second round opponents?
(a) Celtic   (b) Rangers   (c) Aberdeen

4. What was the aggregate score?
(a) 3-0   (b) 5-0   (c) 5-3

5. Who scored a hat-trick in the first leg of the quarter-finals?
(a) Graeme Souness   (b) Kenny Dalglish   (c) David Fairclough

6. Who were the opponents?
(a) Red Star Belgrade   (b) Spartak Moscow   (c) CSKA Sofia

7. Who were the semi-final opponents?
(a) Bayern Munich   (b) Inter Milan   (c) Juventus

8. Who scored Liverpool's only goal of the tie?
(a) Sammy Lee   (b) Ray Kennedy   (c) Graeme Souness

9. Where was the final played?
(a) Nou Camp   (b) San Siro   (c) Parc des Princes.

10. Who were the opponents?
(a) Real Madrid   (b) Bayern Munich   (c) Juventus

11. Who scored Liverpool's only goal of the game?
(a) Ray Kennedy   (b) Alan Kennedy   (c) John F Kennedy

12. Which two Liverpool players finished as the competition's joint top scorers?
(a) Dalglish & Fairclough   (b) Neal & Lee   (c) Souness & McDermott

(Answers p166)

Who Said That? (part 2)

1. "There are those who say maybe I should forget about football. Maybe I should forget about breathing."
(a) Bill Shankly   (b) Gerard Houllier   (c) Rafa Benitez

2. "We have to change, from doubters to believers—now."
(a) Graeme Souness   (b) Bob Paisley   (c) Jurgen Klopp

3. "I want to build a team that's invincible, so that they have to send a team from bloody Mars to beat us."
(a) Bill Shankly   (b) Jurgen Klopp   (c) Graeme Souness

4. "Mind you, I've been here during the bad times too - one year we came second."
(a) Bob Paisley   (b) Kenny Dalglish   (c) Alan Hansen

5. "Cut my veins open and I bleed Liverpool red. I love Liverpool with a burning passion."
(a) Jamie Carragher   (b) Steven Gerrard   (c) Kevin Keegan

6. "I may have left Liverpool but the city and club will always be part of me."
(a) Kevin Keegan   (b) Emlyn Hughes   (c) Kenny Dalglish

7. "We always said we had the best two teams on Merseyside…Liverpool and Liverpool reserves."
(a) Ian St John   (b) Bill Shankly   (c) Bob Paisley

8. "To work hard and have our supporters behind us and believing until the end, you run a little bit more."
(a) Kevin Keegan   (b) Bob Paisley   (c) Rafa Benitez

9. "The difference between Everton and the Queen Mary is that Everton carry more passengers."
(a) Bill Shankly   (b) Tommy Smith   (c) Mark Lawrenson

10. "When you hear Liverpool want you, you call your agent back in about five seconds."
(a) Robbie Fowler   (b) Andy Robertson   (c) Sami Hyypia

(Answers p166)

Liverpool Facts

2018 was a very good year for Mohamed Salah. Here are the eight major awards he picked up.

African Footballer of the Year: 2018
PFA Players' Player of the Year: 2017–18
PFA Fans' Player of the Year: 2017–18
FWA Footballer of the Year: 2017–18
Premier League Player of the Season: 2017–18
Liverpool Fans' Player of the Season Award: 2017–18
Liverpool Players' Player of the Season Award: 2017–18
Premier League Golden Boot: 2017–18

Transfers: The 1970s

Match the following clubs to the Liverpool signings

Arsenal   Ipswich   Partick Thistle
Cardiff   Maccabi Tel Aviv   Scunthorpe
Celtic   Middlesbrough   Skelmersdale
Chesterfield   Newcastle   South Liverpool
Halifax   Newcastle   St. Mirren
Hereford   Northampton   Wrexham
Home Farm   Nottingham Forest

	Date	Player	Fee	Signed from
1	May 1970	Steve Heighway	Free	
2	Nov 1970	John Toshack	£110,000	
3	May 1971	Kevin Keegan	£33,000	
4	Jul 1972	Peter Cormack	£110,000	
5	May 1973	Jimmy Case	£500	
6	Jun 1973	Alan Waddle	£40,000	
7	July 1974	Ray Kennedy	£180,000	
8	Oct 1974	Phil Neal	£66,000	
9	Nov 1974	Terry McDermott	£175,000	
10	Jul 1975	Joey Jones	£110,000	
11	Aug 1976	David Johnson	£200,000	
12	May 1977	Alan Hansen	£100,000	
13	Aug 1977	Kenny Dalglish	£440,000	
14	Nov 1977	Steve Ogrizovic	£70,000	
15	Jan 1978	Graeme Souness	£352,000	
16	Jun 1978	Kevin Sheedy	£80,000	
17	Aug 1978	Alan Kennedy	£330,000	
18	May 1979	Frank McGarvey	£300,000	
19	Jul 1979	Avi Cohen	£200,000	
20	Sep 1979	Ronnie Whelan	Free	

(Answers p167)

Name the season 2

1. Mohamed Sissoko scores his first (and only) goal for the club. Liverpool establish a new record for a Champions League victory after beating Besiktas 8-0. Fernando Torres finishes top scorer in his debut season with 33 goals.

2. Liverpool win a League and Cup double but are knocked out the European Cup by Widzew Łodz..

3. Liverpool are knocked out by Middlesbrough in the semi-final of the League Cup but 18 goals in 36 Premiership games from.a teenage Michael Owen help secure third place.

4. Nine players get on the score-sheet as Liverpool beat Strømsgodset from Norway 11–0 in the Cup Winners' Cup. Liverpool finish second in a record tight season that saw the top ten teams separated by less than ten points.

5. David James signs from Watford for £1million. Liverpool lose 5-1 at Coventry in December. The season ends with a 6-2 win against Spurs.

6. John Barnes signs from Watford. Liverpool go a record 29-matchs unbeaten and win the League with just two defeats

7. Kenny Dalglish departs as manager before the start of the season and is replaced by Brendan Rodgers. Philippe Coutinho signs from Inter. New signing Daniel Sturridge scores a hat-trick in a 6-0 win at St James Park.

8. Liverpool win the League Cup for the first time. Terry McDermott is the season's top scorer.

9. All change at Anfield. Standard Chartered replaces Carlsberg as shirt sponsor. In November new manager Roy Hodgson is replaced by Kenny Dalglish. The following month Tom Werner takes over from Martin Broughton as chairman.

10. Alan Hansen announces his retirement as a player. Steve McManaman makes his debut. Ian Rush and John Barnes are joint top scorers with 16 goals each.

11. Liverpool are knocked out of the European Cup by Red Star Belgrade. Keegan scores twice in the FA Cup final.

(Answers p168)

Robbie Fowler

1. In which Liverpool district was Robbie Fowler born?
(a) Edge Hill   (b) Everton   (c) Toxteth

2. In what season did he make his full Liverpool debut?
(a) 1992-93   (b) 1993-94   (c) 1994-95

3. In the 1994-95 season he scored what was then the Premier League's second-fastest hat-trick. How long did he take?
(a) 4mins 33secs   (b) 6mins 33secs   (c) 8mins 33secs

4. Which award did he win in both 1995 and 1996?
(a) Golden Boot   (b) Liverpool Player of the Year:
(c) PFA Young Player of the Year:

5. Which political cause did Fowler show support for during a goal celebration in 1997?
(a) Liverpool dockers' strike   (b) Irish Independence
(c) Anti-apartheid

6. What type of injury forced him to miss the 1998 World Cup Finals?
(a) achilles   (b) knee   (c) groin

7. How many times did he win the FA Cup?
(a) none   (b) one   (c) two

8. How many full England caps did he earn?
(a) 26   (b) 46   (c) 66

9. How many goals did he score for Liverpool?
(a) 151   (b) 171   (c) 191

10. How many appearances did he make for Liverpool?
(a) 270   (b) 300   (c) 330

11. How many goals did he score in Liverpool's 5-0 defeat of Fulham in the League Cup in October 1993?
(a) three   (b) four   (c) five

12. Which club did he sign for after leaving Liverpool in 2001?
(a) Newcastle   (b) Leeds   (c) Sheffield Wednesday

13. What was the transfer fee?
(a) £8 million   (b) £10 million   (c) £12 million

14. Which former Liverpool player was Fowler's manager from 2003 to 2005?
(a) John Toshack   (b) Graeme Souness   (c) Kevin Keegan

15. Which was the last English club he played for?
(a) Blackburn   (b) Leeds   (c) Cardiff

(Answers p168)

Where are they from? (part 2)

Fill in the players' countries of birth below

	Player	Years at club	Country of birth
1	Avi Cohen	1979–81	
2	Craig Johnston	1981–88	
3	Bruce Grobbelaar	1981–94	
4	Jim Beglin	1983–89	
5	Jan Molby	1984–96	
6	Glenn Hysen	1989–92	
7	Ronny Rosenthal	1990–94	
8	Torben Piechnik	1992-94	
9	Stig Inge Bjornebye	1992–00	
10	Phil Babb	1994–00	
11	Patrik Berger	1996–03	
12	Karl-Heinz Riedle	1997–99	
13	Bjorn Tore Kvarme	1997–99	
14	Oyvind Leonhardsen	1997–99	
15	Brad Friedel	1997–00	
16	Rigobert Song	1999–00	
17	Titi Camara	1999–00	
18	Sander Westerveld	1999–01	
19	Vladimír Šmicer	1999–05	
20	Stéphane Henchoz	1999–05	

(Answers p169)

Shoot-outs 4

2005 Champions League. Final
Ataturk Stadium, Wed 25 May
AC Milan 3 - 3 **Liverpool**

Line-up: Jerzy Dudek, Steve Finnan, Sami Hyypia, John Arne Riise,
Djimi Traore, Jamie Carragher, Harry Kewell, Steven Gerrard (capt),
Luis Garcia, Xabi Alonso, Milan Baros
Subs: Vladimir Smicer, Didi Hamann, Djibril Cisse

Fill in the names of Liverpool's penalty takers below

	Liverpool			Milan	
			0 - 0	Serginho	missed
1		scored	1 - 0		
			1 - 0	Andrea Pirlo	saved
2		scored	2 - 0		
			2 - 1	Jon Dahl Tomasson	scored
3		saved	2 - 1		
			2 - 2	Kaka	scored
4		scored	3 - 2		
			3 - 2	Andriy Shevchenko	saved

(Answers p169)

Jurgen Klopp

1. Where was Jurgen Klopp born?
(a) Stuttgart (b) Dresden (c) Frankfurt

2. What year was he born?
(a) 1965 (b) 1967 (c) 1969

3. What did he want to be as a young boy?
(a) an architect (b) a doctor (c) a dentist

4. Which club did he play for from 1990 to 2001?
(a) Wolfsburg (b) FC Schalke 04 (c) Mainz 05

5. How tall is he?
(a) 6ft (b) 6ft 2 (c) 6ft 4

6. Which was the first club he managed?
(a) Mainz 05 (b) Leipzig (c) Schalke 04

7. Which club did he manage before taking charge of Liverpool?
(a) Borussia Monchengladbach (b) Stuttgart (c) Borussia Dortmund

8. How many times did he win the Bundesliga as a manager?
(a) one (b) two (c) three

9. What year did he become Liverpool manager?
(a) 2014 (b) 2015 (c) 2016

10. What is his middle name?
(a) Emmett (b) Karl (c) Norbert

11. Who was his first signing as Liverpool manager?
(a) Marko Grujic (b) Loris Karius (c) Kamil Grabara.

12. Where did he meet his current wife?
(a) at a football game (b) at an Oktoberfest (c) at a knockwurst convention

13. Who was Klopp's most expensive signing?
(a) Alisson Becker (b) Mohamed Salah (c) Virgil Van Dijk

14. For which car manufacturer is he a "brand ambassador"?
(a) Opel (b) Volkswagen (c) BMW

15. Who were the opponents when Klopp was charged with misconduct after running onto the pitch to celebrate a 96th minute winner in December 2018?
(a) Man City (b) Arsenal (c) Everton

(Answers p170)

Name the Six...

... Clubs that Liverpool beat in European Cup & Champions League finals

1 _____ (1977)

2 _____ (1978)

3 _____ (1981)

4 _____ (1984)

5 _____ (2005)

6 _____ (2019).

... Liverpool players who have won BBC's Goal of the Season award

1 _____ (1976-77)

2 _____ (1978-79)

3 _____ (1987-88 & 1988-89)

4 _____ (2003-04)

5 _____ (2005-06)

6 _____ (2016-17)

... Players who have scored for Liverpool since January 2008 whose full names start and end with the same letter (e.g Robbie FowleR)

1 _____

2 _____

3 _____

4 _____

5 _____

6 _____

(Answers p170)

Anagrams 2

Rearrange the letters to form the names of famous Liverpool players. The years they were at the club are in brackets.

(1) Playgirl siege   _ _ _ _ / _ _ _ _ _ _ _ _ _
(1983–1991)

(2) Manly job   _ _ _ / _ _ _ _ _
(1984–1996)

(3) Caveman sent mam   _ _ _ _ _ / _ _ _ _ _ _ _ _ _
(1990–1999)

(4) Borrow belief   _ _ _ _ _ _ / _ _ _ _ _ _
(1993–2001)

(5) Chilean meow   _ _ _ _ _ _ _ / _ _ _ _
(1996–2004)

(6) Alien cup   _ _ _ _ / _ _ _ _
(1997–1999)

(7) Denver garters   _ _ _ _ _ _ / _ _ _ _ _ _ _
(1998–2015)

(8) Slimmer Jane   _ _ _ _ _ / _ _ _ _ _ _
(2015–)

(9) Asian dome   _ _ _ _ _ / _ _ _ _
    (2016–)

(10) Bonny roadster   _ _ _ _ / _ _ _ _ _ _ _ _ _
     (2017–)

(Answers p171)

Liverpool Facts

Ian Rush scored hat-tricks for Liverpool in six different competitions: the League, FA Cup, League Cup, European Cup, Cup Winners' Cup and Super Cup.

Rush always enjoyed a happy New Year. He played seven times for Liverpool on New Year's Day and scored on every occasion.

The 1983–84 European Cup

1. Who were Liverpool's first round opponents?
(a) Odense   (b) Linfield   (c) Vllaznia

2. What was the aggregate score?
(a) 4-0   (b) 6-0   (c) 8-0

3. In which Spanish city did Liverpool play the second round second leg?
(a) Vienna   (b) Prague   (c) Bilbao

4. Who scored Liverpool's only goal of the tie?
(a) Ian Rush   (b) Kenny Dalglish   (c) Graeme Souness

5. Who were Liverpool's quarter-final opponents?
(a) Rapid Vienna   (b) Benfica   (c) Dundee United

6. Who scored twice in the 4-1 win away in the second leg?
(a) Craig Johnson   (b) Ian Rush   (c) Ronny Whelan

7. In which city was the second leg of the quarter-finals played?
(a) Tbilisi   (b) Bucharest   (c) Moscow

8. Who scored both Liverpool goals in the 2-1 win there?
(a) Ian Rush   (b) Kenny Dalglish   (c) Graeme Souness

9. In which Italian stadium was the final played?
(a) Stadio Flaminio   (b) Stadio Olimpico (c) Stadio Artemio Franchi

10. What was the attendance?

(a) 60,000   (b) 70,000   (c) 80,000

11. Who scored Liverpool's only goal of the game?

(a) Steve Nicol   (b) Alan Kennedy   (c) Phil Neal

12. Who missed Roma's final penalty?

(a) Francesco Graziani   (b) Bruno Conti   (c) Michele Nappi

(Answers p171)

Emlyn Hughes

1. Where was Emlyn Hughes born?
(a) Barrow-in-Furness   (b) Southport   (c) Carlisle

2. What professional sport did his father, Fred, play?
(a) football   (b) cricket   (c) rugby league

3. What was the first club he played for?
(a) Blackpool   (b) Southport   (c) Brighton

4. What was the transfer fee when he signed for Liverpool in 1967?
(a) £35,000   (b) £65,000   (c) £95,000

5. How many appearances did he make for Liverpool?
(a) 565   (b) 665   (c) 765

6. How many goals did he score for Liverpool?
(a) 29   (b) 39   (c) 49

7. What nickname did he earn at Liverpool?
 (a) Trigger   (b) Crazy Horse   (c) Red Rum

8. How many full England caps did he earn?
(a) 42   (b) 52   (c) 62

9. How many games did he play in the World Cup finals?
(a) none   (b) four   (c) eight

10. How many League Titles did he win with Liverpool as captain?
(a) two   (b) three   (c) four

11. Who did he sign for after leaving Liverpool in 1979?
(a) Wolves   (b) Aston Villa   (c) West Brom

12. Who was his opposing captain when he first appeared on BBC's *A Question of Sport* in 1979?
(a) Bill Beaumont   (b) Willie Carson   (c) Gareth Edwards

13. At what club did he finish his playing career?
(a) Hull City   (b) Stoke City   (c) Swansea City

14. Which club did he manage between 1981 and 1983?
(a) Rotherham   (b) Mansfield   (c) Blackpool

15. What honour was he awarded in 1980?
(a) MBE   (b) OBE   (c) CBE

(Answers p172)

Shoot-outs 5

2006 FA Cup Final
Millennium Stadium, Sat 13 May
Liverpool 3 - 3 West Ham

Line-up: Pepe Reina, Steve Finnan, Sami Hyypia,John Arne Riise, Jamie Carragher, Harry Kewell, Steven Gerrard (capt), Xabi Alonso, Momo Sissoko, Djibril Cisse, Peter Crouch.
Subs: Fernando Morientes, Jan Kromkamp, Didi Hamann

Fill in in the names of Liverpool's penalty takers below

	Liverpool			West Ham	
1		scored	1 - 0		
			1 - 0	Bobby Zamora	saved
2		saved	1 - 0		
			1 - 1	Teddy Sheringham	scored
3		scored	2 - 1		
			2 - 1	Paul Konchesky	saved
4		scored	3 - 1		
			3 - 1	Anton Ferdinand	saved

(Answers p172)

76

Transfers: The 1980s

Match the following clubs to the Liverpool signings:

Ajax Coventry Oxford
Aston Villa Fiorentina Shamrock Rovers
Ayr United Ipswich Town Sunderland
Brighton Luton Town Vancouver Whitecaps
Brighton Middlesbrough Watford
Chelsea Newcastle West Brom
Chester Oxford

	Date	Player	Fee	Signed from
1	Apr 1980	Ian Rush	£300,000	
2	Mar 1981	Bruce Grobbelaar	£250,000	
3	Apr 1981	Craig Johnston	£650,000	
4	Aug 1981	Mark Lawrenson	£900,000	
5	Oct 1981	Steve Nicol	£300,000	
6	May 1983	Jim Beglin	£20,000	
7	Jul 1983	Gary Gillespie	£325,000	
8	Aug 1983	Michael Robinson	£200,000	
9	Mar 1984	John Wark	£475,000	
10	May 1984	Paul Walsh	£700,000	
11	Aug 1984	Jan Molby	£200,000	
12	Sep 1985	Steve McMahon	£350,000	
13	Jul 1986	Barry Venison	£200,000	
14	Jan 1987	John Aldridge	£750,000	
15	Feb 1987	Nigel Spackman	£400,000	
16	Jun 1987	John Barnes	£900,000	
17	Jul 1987	Peter Beardsley	£1,900,000	
18	Oct 1987	Ray Houghton	£825,000	
19	Oct 1988	David Burrows	£550,000	
20	Jul 1989	Glenn Hysen	£600,000	

Select the clubs that players moved to from Liverpool

Bolton	Minnesota Kicks	Sheffield United
Brighton	Newcastle	Sunderland
Everton	QPR	Swansea
Juventus	QPR	Tottenham
Lucerne	QPR	Tottenham
Luton	Real Sociedad	Wolves
Maccabi Tel Aviv	Sampdoria	

	Date	Player	Fee	Went to
1	Aug 1979	Emlyn Hughes	£90,000	
2	April 1981	Steve Heighway	Free	
3	Aug 1981	Ray Clemence	£300,000	
4	Aug 1981	Jimmy Case	£350,000	
5	Nov 1981	Avi Cohen	£100,000	
6	Jan 1982	Ray Kennedy	£160,000	
7	Apr 1982	Richard Money	£100,000	
8	Aug 1982	David Johnson	£100,000	
9	Sep 1982	Terry McDermott	£100,000	
10	Jul 1983	David Fairclough	Free	
11	Jun 1984	Graeme Souness	£650,000	
12	Dec 1984	Michael Robinson	£100,000	
13	Mar1985	Phil Thompson	Free	
14	Sep 1985	Alan Kennedy	£100,000	
15	Dec 1985	Phil Neal	Free	
16	Aug 1986	Sammy Lee	£200,000	
17	Jul 1987	Ian Rush	£3,200,000	
18	Feb 1988	Paul Walsh	£500,000	
19	Feb 1989	Nigel Spackman	£500,000	
20	Sep 1989	John Aldridge	£1,250,000	

(Answers p173)

Name the season 3

1. Liverpool start the season with two managers but end it with one. There are fourth round exits in both domestic cups, while a seventh place finish means Liverpool fail to qualify for European football for the first time in five seasons.

2. In Gerard Houllier's last in charge Liverpool suffer two fourth round cup exits and finish fourth in the Premier League.

3. Sadio Mane signs from Southampton before the start of the season. Liverpool field the youngest starting XI in their history in the FA Cup third tie at Plymouth. James Milner misses a penalty in a 0-0 draw against Southampton, the fourth time Liverpool had failed to score against the south coast club that season.

4. A Peter Cormack goal against Crystal Palace makes it 21 consecutive home wins in the league, the longest run in English top-flight history until it was surpassed by Jurgen Klopp's side in 2020. Kevin Keegan and John Toshack are joint top scorers with 13 League goals each.

5. Craig Bellamy makes his debut in the third qualifying round of the Champions League against Maccabi Haifa. Bellamy also scores in the 2-1 win at the Nou Camp in the round of 16.

6. Liverpool are knocked out of the European Cup in the first round, but Ray Clemence's 28 clean sheets help secure the League with a record points total.

7. Bruce Grobbelaar, Steve Nicol and Ronnie Whelan all leave on free transfers. Liverpool start the season with a 6-1 away win. Steve McManaman scores two crucial goals in April.

8. Michael Owen departs for Real Madrid while Djibril Cisse joins from Auxerre. The season ends on a glorious note

9. All change for the start of this season. New signing Sander Westerveld replaces the outgoing David James, while Stephane Henchoz and Sami Hyypiä form a new central defensive partnership. In March Emile Heskey is signed from Leicester for a club record £11 million.

10. Man City's Mario Balotelli is sent off at Anfield 15 minutes after coming off the bench. A Steven Gerrard penalty gives Liverpool a 1-0 first leg victory against City in the League Cup semi-final. In his 400th league appearance Gerrard scores all the goals in the 3–0 victory over Everton.

11. Pepe Reina signs in the summer and becomes Liverpool's first-choice keeper. His final touch of the season is to save an Anton Ferdinand penalty.

(Answers p174)

Who am I? (part 2)

1. I became the most expensive teenager in British football history when I moved to Liverpool in 1995. My later clubs include Wimbledon and Wolves

2. Born in 1966, I helped beat Liverpool in an FA Cup final. I played 94 games for Liverpool before being sold to Tottenham.

3. I played for three London clubs before moving to the south coast. Before joining Liverpool I won Goal of the Season. I've been capped 54 times by England.

4. I'm a World Cup winner who was born in Fuenlabrada. I played 142 times for Liverpool before moving to London.

5. I joined Liverpool from Ajax and played in the centre of the defence before moving into midfield. Of the 62 goals I scored for the club, 42 were from penalties.

6. I spent eight seasons in the lower leagues before joining Liverpool. I scored 422 goals in my career including 40 in Spain.

7. I speak four languages fluently: Swahili, English, Dutch, and French. I played on loan in Germany whilst at Liverpool, but returned to score a special European goal.

8. I joined the Sunderland academy aged eight and went on to play for the first team. A year after joining Liverpool I won they won the League Cup. I've played in midfield and defence.

9. I've played for seven Premier League clubs and signed for Liverpool twice. I'm rumoured to have a wild golf swing.

10. I was born in Molde and joined Liverpool from Monaco. I left the city for Rome with a Champions League winner's medal.

(Answers p174)

Liverpool Facts

Ian Callaghan is Liverpool's best-behaved player. In his 857 games for the club he was only booked once.

In September 1982, Liverpool scored against three different Luton Town goalkeepers in a league game at Anfield. Back then there was no substitute keeper, so after the Luton goalkeeper went off injured their full-back and centre-half took it in turns to keep goal.

Bill Shankly

1. What year was Bill Shankly born?
(a) 1908   (b) 1913   (c) 1918

2. Where was he born?
(a) Bellshill, North Lanarkshire   (b) Dundee
(c) Glenbuck, Ayrshire

3. What job did he do after leaving school?
(a) miner   (b) delivery man   (c) steel worker

4. How many of his brothers played professional football?
(a) none   (b) two   (c) four

5. Which club did he play for from 1933 to 1949?
(a) Preston North End   (b) Rotherham   (c) Stoke City

6. What position did he play?
(a) centre-half   (b) right-half   (c) centre-forward

7. What was his salary after joining them?
(a) £5 a week   (b) £15 a week   (c) £30 a week

8. Which branch of the armed forces did he serve with in the Second World War?
(a) Army   (b) Navy   (c) Air Force

9. Which club did he first manage?
(a) Doncaster   (b) Carlisle   (c) Port Vale

10. Which club did he manage before taking charge at Liverpool?
(a) Huddersfield   (b) Crewe   (c) Burnley

11. What year did he become Liverpool manager?
(a) 1957   (b) 1959   (c) 1961

12. How many League titles did he win at Liverpool?
(a) one   (b) two   (c) three

13. How many FA Cups did he win?
(a) one   (b) two   (c) three

14. Which European trophy did he win at Liverpool?
(a) Uefa Cup   (b) European Cup   (c) Cup Winners Cup

15. What was his last game in charge of Liverpool?
(a) Charity Shield   (b) Uefa Cup final   (c) FA Cup final

(Answers p175)

Name the Seven...

... Brazilians who have played for Liverpool in the Premier League

1 _____

2 _____

3 _____

4 _____

5 _____

6 _____

7 _____

... Germans who have played for Liverpool in the Premier League

1 _____

2 _____

3 _____

4 _____

5 _____

6 _____

7 _____

... Players who have played for Liverpool in the Premier League whose surname end in a double letter

1 _____

2 _____

3 _____

4 _____

5 _____

6 _____

7 _____

Seasons when Liverpool won the FA Cup

1 _____

2 _____

3 _____

4 _____

5 _____

6 _____

7 _____

(Answers p175)

How Tall? (part 3)

	Player	Years at club	Height
1	Alan Hansen	1977–1991	
2	Alan Kennedy	1978–1986	
3	Graeme Souness	1978–1984	
4	Ronnie Whelan	1979–1994	
5	Ian Rush	1980–1986	
6	Bruce Grobbelaar	1981–1994	
7	Mark Lawrenson	1981–1988	
8	Steve Nicol	1981–1994	
9	Craig Johnston	1981–1988	
10	Gary Gillespie	1983–1991	
11	Jan Mølby	1984–1996	
12	Ray Houghton	1987–1992	
13	David Burrows	1988–1993	
14	Steve McManaman	1990–1999	
15	Rob Jones	1991–1999	
16	Mark Wright	1991–1998	
17	Michael Thomas	1991–1998	
18	Robbie Fowler	1993–2001	
19	Patrik Berger	1996–2003	
20	Jamie Carragher	1996–2013	

Score half a point if you're an inch out either way. Half inches are rounded up.

(Answers p176)

Shoot-outs 6

2007 Champions League. Semi-final 2nd leg
Anfield, Tue 1 May
Liverpool 1 - 0 Chelsea

Line-up: Pepe Reina, Steve Finnan, Daniel Agger, John Arne Riise, Jamie Carragher, Steven Gerrard (capt), Jermaine Pennant , Javier Mascherano, Bolo Zenden, Peter Crouch, Dirk Kuyt.
Subs: Xabi Alonso, Craig Bellamy, Robbie Fowler

Fill in Liverpool's penalty takers below

	Liverpool			Chelsea	
1		Scored	1 – 0		
			1 – 0	Arjen Robben	saved
2		Scored	2 – 0		
			2 – 1	Frank Lampard	scored
3		Scored	3 – 1		
			3 – 1	Geremi	saved
4		Scored	4 – 1		

(Answers p177)

Transfers: The 1990s

Match the following clubs to the Liverpool signings

Arsenal	Derby	Rosenborg
Bolton	Marseille	Tottenham
Borussia Dortmund	Millwall	Vitesse Arnhem
Bournemouth	Newcastle	Watford
Columbus Crew	Notts Forest	Willem II
Coventry	Notts Forest	Wimbledon
Crewe	Rangers	

	Date	Player	Fee	Signed from
1	Jan 1991	Jamie Redknapp	£350,000	
2	Jul 1991	Dean Saunders	£2,900,000	
3	Aug 1991	Mark Walters	£1,250,000	
4	Oct 1991	Rob Jones	£300,000	
5	Dec 1991	Michael Thomas	£1,500,000	
6	Jun 1992	David James	£1,000,000	
7	Dec 1992	Stig Inge Bjornebye	£600,000	
8	Jun 1993	Nigel Clough	£2,275,000	
9	Jul 1993	Neil Ruddock	£2,500,000	
10	Sep 1994	Phil Babb	£3,600,000	
11	Sep 1994	John Scales	£3,500,000	
12	Mar 1995	Mark Kennedy	£1,500,000	
13	Jul 1995	Stan Collymore	£8,500,000	
14	Sep 1995	Jason McAteer	£4,500,000	
15	Jul 1997	Karl-Heinz Riedle	£1,800,000	
16	Dec 1997	Brad Friedel	£1,000,000	
17	May 1999	Sami Hyypia	£2,500,000	
18	Jun 1999	Titi Camara	£2,600,000	
19	Jun 1999	Sander Westerveld	£4,000,000	
20	Jul 1999	Didi Hamann	£8,000,000	

Select the clubs that players moved to from Liverpool

Aston Villa   **Everton**   **Saint-Etienne**
Aston Villa   **Man City**   **Southampton**
Aston Villa   **Man City**   **Swansea**
Aston Villa   **Newcastle**   **Tottenham**
Blackburn   **Newcastle**   **Wimbledon**
Blackburn   **Notts County**   **West Ham**
Celtic   **Real Madrid**

	Date	Player	Fee	Went to
1	Aug 1991	Steve Staunton	£1,100,000	
2	Aug 1991	Gary Gillespie	£900,000	
3	Aug 1991	David Speedie	£500,000	
4	Dec 1991	Steve McMahon	£900,000	
5	Jan 1992	Gary Ablett	£750,000	
6	Jul 1992	Barry Venison	£250,000	
7	Jul 1992	Ray Houghton	£825,000	
8	Jan 1995	Steve Nicol	Free	
9	Jan 1996	Mark Walters	Free	
10	Jan 1996	Nigel Clough	£1,500,000	
11	Feb 1996	Jan Molby	Free	
12	Dec 1996	John Scales	£2,600,000	
13	May 1997	Stan Collymore	£7,000,000	
14	Aug 1997	John Barnes	Free	
15	Mar 1998	Mark Kennedy	£1,750,000	
16	Jul 1998	Neil Ruddock	£400,000	
17	Jan 1999	Jason McAteer	£4,000,000	
18	Jun 1999	David James	£1,800,000	
19	Jul 1999	Steve McManaman	Free	
20	Aug 1999	Bjorn Tore Kvarme	£750,000	

(Answers p177)

The 2004-05 Champions League

1. Who did Liverpool defeat in the third qualifying round?
(a) Baník Ostrava   (b) Grazer AK   (c) Shelbourne

2. Who did Liverpool defeat 3-1 in the final group game to reach the round of 16?
(a) Deportivo de La Coruna   (b) Dynamo Kyiv
(c) Olympiacos

3. Who finished top of Liverpool's group?
(a) Monaco   (b) Lyon   (c) PSG

4. Who scored in both legs of the round of 16?
(a) Luis Garcia   (b) Steven Gerrard   (c) Xabi Alonso

5. Who were the opponents?
(a) PSV Eindhoven   (b) Werder Bremen   (c) Bayer Leverkusen

6. What was the aggregate score?
(a) 3-2   (b) 5-1   (c) 6-2

7. Who scored Liverpool's opening goal in the first leg of the quarter-finals?
(a) Milan Baros   (b) Sami Hyypia   (c) John Arne Riise

8. Who were the opponents?
(a) Juventus   (b) Inter Milan   (c) Lyon

9. What was the score in the first leg of the semi-final at Stamford Bridge?
(a) 0-0   (b) 1-1   (c) 2-2

10. Who scored the only goal of the second leg?
(a) Luis García   (b) Steven Gerrard   (c) Xabi Alonso

11. What was the time of the goal?
(a) 2mins   (b) 4mins   (c) 6mins

12. How much injury time was awarded at the end of the second half?
(a) 2mins   (b) 4mins   (c) 6mins

13. What was the Turkish name of the stadium where the final took place?
(a) Türk Telekom Stadı   (b) Atatürk Stadı   (c) Atatürk Olimpiyat Stadı

14. What was the attendance?
(a) 68,059   (b) 72,059   (c) 76,059

15. Who scored Milan's opening goal?
(a) Paolo Maldini   (b) Hernan Crespo   (c) Andrea Pirlo

16. How much time had been played?
(a) 1min   (b) 2mins   (c) 3mins

17. Who scored Liverpool's second goal?
(a) John Arne Riise   (b) Vladimir Smicer   (c) Steven Gerrard

18. When did Alonso score Liverpool's equaliser?
(a) 60mins   (b) 65mins   (c) 70mins

19. Who scored Liverpool's opening penalty?
(a) Djibril Cisse   (b) Xabi Alonso   (c) Dietmar Hamann

20. Who missed the penalty that secured Liverpool the trophy?
(a) Andrea Pirlo   (b) Andriy Shevchenko   (c) Kaka

(Answers p178)

Liverpool Facts

In 2014-15 Steven Gerrard beat Billy Liddell's record, set in 1960, by scoring for Liverpool in 16 successive seasons.

The Merseyside derby between Liverpool and Everton might be known as "The Friendly Derby" but it has actually produced more red cards than any other fixture in the league.

Who Said That? (part 3)

1. "We don't destroy our heroes today when we worshipped them yesterday."
(a) Gerard Houllier   (b) Bill Shankly   (c) Kenny Dalglish

2. "I don't think I was ever smart enough for a medical career."
(a) Emlyn Hughes   (b) Rafa Benitez   (c) Jurgen Klopp

3. "If you are first, you are first. If you are second…you are nothing."
(a) Bill Shankly   (b) Kevin Keegan   (c) Kenny Dalglish

4. "There is no one anywhere in the world at any stage who is any bigger or any better than this football club."
(a) Bob Paisley   (b) Kenny Dalglish   (c) Steven Gerrard

5. "Liverpool without European football is like a banquet without wine."
(a) Kevin Keegan   (b) Roy Evans   (c) Phil Thompson

6. "Some people believe football is a matter of life and death, I am very disappointed with that attitude. I can assure you it is much, much more important than that."
(a) Gerard Houllier   (b) Alan Hansen   (c) Bill Shankly

7. "Liverpool are magic. Everton are tragic."
(a) Emlyn Hughes   (b) Tommy Smith   (c) Robbie Fowler

8. "The whole of my life, what they (Liverpool supporters) wanted was honesty. They were not concerned with cultured football, but with triers who gave one hundred percent."
(a) Kevin Keegan   (b) Bill Shankly   (c) Bob Paisley

9. "The Anfield atmosphere is difficult to explain, you just have to experience it. Every player should try it at least once in his career."
(a) Peter Crouch   (b) Milan Baros   (c) Alvaro Arbeloa

10. "They compare Steve McManaman to Steve Heighway and he's nothing like him, but I can see why - it's because he's a bit different."
(a) Mark Lawrenson   (b) Kevin Keegan   (c) Alan Hansen

(Answers p179)

Alan Hansen

1. From which Scandianavian country does his surname originate?
(a) Denmark   (b) Norway   (c) Sweden

2. How did he get the scar on his forehead, aged 15?
(a) in a car accident   (b) playing ruby   (c) he ran into a plate-glass panel

3. What sport did he want to take up professionally between the ages of 15 and 17?
(a) hockey   (b) golf   (c) snooker

4. Who did he play for before joining Liverpool?
(a) Kilmarnock   (b) Partick Thistle   (c) Dundee United

5. What was the transfer fee when he signed for Liverpool in 1977?
(a) £110,000   (b) £210,000   (c) £310,000

6. How many appearances did he make for Liverpool?
(a) 420   (b) 520   (c) 620

7. What was his nickname at Anfield?
(a) Rocky   (b) Jockey   (c) Stretch

8. How many goals did he score for Liverpool?
(a) 7   (b) 14   (c) 21

9. How many Titles did he win with Liverpool?
(a) six   (b) seven   (c) eight

10. How many full Scotland caps did he earn?
(a) 26   (b) 46   (c) 66

11. In what year was he made Liverpool captain?
(a) 1982   (b) 1985   (c) 1988

12. How tall is he?
(a) 6ft   (b) 6ft 2   (c) 6ft 4

13. How many European Cups did he win?
(a) one   (b) two   (c) three

14. For how many years was he pundit on *Match of the Day*?
(a) 12   (b) 16   (c) 22

15. What is the title of his autobiography?
(a) Tall, Dark and Hansen   (b) You Hansen Devil   (c) In My Liverpool Home

(Answers p180)

Name the Eight...

... Liverpool players to be named PFA Player of the Season

1 _____ (1979-80)

2 _____ (1982-83)

3 _____ (1983-84)

4 _____ (1987-88)

5 _____ (2005-06)

6 _____ (2013-14)

7 _____ (2017-18)

8 _____ (2018-19).

... Seasons when Liverpool won the League Cup

1 _____

2 _____

3 _____

4 _____

5 _____

6 _____

7 _____

8 _____

(Answers p180)

Where are they from? (part 3)

Fill in the players' countries of birth below

	Player	Years at club	Country of birth
1	Djimi Traore	1999–06	
2	Dietmar Hamann	1999–06	
3	Sami Hyypia	1999–09	
4	Christian Ziege	2000–01	
5	Markus Babbel	2000–04	
6	Jari Litmanen	2001–02	
7	Nicolas Anelka	2001–02	
8	Florent Pongolle	2001–06	
9	John Arne Riise	2001–08	
10	Jerzy Dudek	2001–07	
11	El Hadji Diouf	2002–05	
12	Milan Baros	2002–05	
13	Harry Kewell	2003–08	
14	Luis García	2004–07	
15	Djibril Cisse	2004–07	
16	Xabi Alonso	2004–09	
17	Mohamed Sissoko	2005–08	
18	Fernando Morientes	2005–06	
19	Pepe Reina	2005–14	
20	Dirk Kuyt	2006–12	

(Answers p181)

Shoot-outs 7

2012 League Cup Final
Wembley, Sun 26 Feb
Liverpool 2 - 2 **Cardiff City**

Line-up: Pepe Reina, Glen Johnson, Jose Enrique, Daniel Agger, Martin Skrtel, Steven Gerrard (capt), Jordan Henderson, Stewart Downing, Charlie Adam, Luis Suarez, Andy Carroll
Subs: Craig Bellamy, Jamie Carragher, Dirk Kuyt

Fill in Liverpool's penalty takers below

	Liverpool			Cardiff	
1		Missed	0 - 0		
			0 - 0	Kenny Miller	missed
2		Missed	0 - 0		
			0 - 1	Don Cowie	scored
3		Scored	1 - 1		
			1 - 1	Rudy Gestede	missed
4		Scored	2 - 1		
			2 - 2	Peter Whittingham	scored
5		Scored	3 - 2		
			3 - 2	Anthony Gerrard	missed

(Answers p181)

Transfers: The 2000s

Match the following clubs to the Liverpool signings

Atletico Madrid	Feyenoord	Portsmouth
Auxerre	Leeds	Real Sociedad
Banik Ostrava	Leicester	Southampton
Barcelona	Lens	Valencia
Blackburn	Middlesbrough	Villarreal
Brondby	Monaco	Zenit St Petersburg
Coventry	Paris St Germain	

	Date	Player	Fee	Signed from
1	Mar 2000	Emile Heskey	£11,000,000	
2	Aug 2000	Christian Ziege	£5,500,000	
3	Jun 2001	John Arne Riise	£4,000,000	
4	Jul 2001	Milan Baros	£3,200,000	
5	Aug 2001	Chris Kirkland	£6,000,000	
6	Jun 2002	El Hadji Diouf	£10,000,000	
7	Jul 2003	Harry Kewell	£5,000,000	
8	Jul 2004	Djibril Cisse	£14,500,000	
9	Aug 2004	Xabi Alonso	£10,700,000	
10	Aug 2004	Luis Garcia	£6,000,000	
11	Jul 2005	Pepe Reina	£6,000,000	
12	Jul 2005	Momo Sissoko	£5,600,000	
13	Jul 2005	Peter Crouch	£7,000,000	
14	Jan 2006	Daniel Agger	£5,800,000	
15	Jul 2006	Craig Bellamy	£6,000,000	
16	Aug 2006	Dirk Kuyt	£9,000,000	
17	Jul 2007	Fernando Torres	£20,200,000	
18	Jan 2008	Martin Skrtel	£6,500,000	
19	Jul 2008	David N'Gog	£1,500,000	
20	Jun 2009	Glen Johnson	£17,500,000	

Select the clubs that players moved to from Liverpool

Aston Villa	Bordeaux	Portsmouth
Aston Villa	Charlton	Real Madrid
Atletico Madrid	Charlton	Real Sociedad
Birmingham	Espanyol	Tottenham
Blackburn	Juventus	Tottenham
Bolton	Leeds	West Ham
Bolton	Marseille	

	Date	Player	Fee	Went to
1	Jun 2000	Stig Inge Bjornebye	£300,000	
2	Dec 2000	Steve Staunton	Free	
3	Nov 2001	Robbie Fowler	£12,000,000	
4	Dec 2001	Sander Westerveld	£3,750,000	
5	Apr 2002	Jamie Redknapp	Free	
6	May 2004	Emile Heskey	£6,250,000	
7	Aug 2004	Danny Murphy	£2,500,000	
8	Aug 2004	Michael Owen	£8,500,000	
9	Jun 2005	Vladimir Smicer	Free	
10	Jun 2005	El Hadji Diouf	£3,500,000	
11	Aug 2005	Milan Baros	£6,500,000	
12	Jul 2006	Didi Hamann	Free	
13	Aug 2006	Djimi Traore	£2,000,000	
14	Jul 2007	Luis Garcia	£4,000,000	
15	Jul 2007	Djibril Cisse	£6,000,000	
16	Jul 2007	Craig Bellamy	£7,500,000	
17	Jan 2008	Momo Sissoko	£8,200,000	
18	Jul 2008	Peter Crouch	£11,000,000	
19	Aug 2008	Steve Finnan	Undisclosed	
20	Feb 2009	Robbie Keane	£16,000,000	

(Answers p182)

Steven Gerrard

1. What year was Steven Gerrard born?
(a) 1978   (b) 1980   (c) 1982

2. In what season did he make his Liverpool debut?
(a) 1998-99   (b) 1999-00   (c) 2000-01

3. How many Champions League goals has he scored?
(a) 15   (b) 30   (c) 45

4. In what year did he turn down a £20 million offer from Chelsea?
(a) 2003   (b) 2004   (c) 2005

5. How many FA Cups did he win?
(a) one   (b) two   (c) three

6. Who did he replace as Liverpool captain in October 2003?
(a) Michael Owen   (b) Dietmar Hamann   (c) Sami Hyypia

7. How many games did he play as captain?
(a) 273   (b) 373   (c) 473

8. How tall is he ?
(a) 5ft 10   (b) 5ft 11   (c) 6ft

9. How many goals did he score in Liverpool's successful 2004-05 Champions League campaign?
(a) two   (b) four   (c) six

10. In what minute of the 2005 Champions League final did Gerrard score?
(a) 54th   (b) 58th   (c) 62nd

11. Who were the opponents when Gerrard scored an own goal in the 2005 League Cup final?
(a) Arsenal   (b) Chelsea   (c) Tottenham

12. How many appearances did he make for Liverpool?
(a) 510   (b) 610   (c) 710

13. How many goals did he score for Liverpool?
(a) 146   (b) 186   (c) 226

14. How many full England caps did he earn?
(a) 74   (b) 94   (c) 114

15. Which MLS club did he join in 2015?
(a) LA Galaxy   (b) Chicago Fire   (c) D.C. United

(Answers p183)

Who wins at Scrabble?

Name the five players in the current Liverpool squad whose names would produce the highest Scrabble score.

1. _____ 45 points

2. _____ 37 points

3. _____ 33 points

4. _____ 32 points

5. _____ 29 points

And which names would produce the lowest?

1. _____ 7 points

2. _____ 7 points

3. _____ 10 points

4. _____ 12 points

5. _____ 15 points

How to score:
1 point: A E I L N O R S T U
2 points: D G
3 points: B C M P
4 points: F H V W Y.
5 points: K
8 points: J X
10 points Q Z

(Answers p184)

The 2018-19 Champions League

1. Who scored Liverpool's first goal of the campaign?
(a) James Milner   (b) Daniel Sturridge   (c) Sadio Mane

2. In which minute of injury time did Firmino score the winner in the opening group game v Paris Saint-Germain?
(a) 2nd   (b) 3rd   (c) 4th

3. Who did Liverpool lose 2-0 to in the fourth game?
(a) PSG   (b) Napoli   (c) Red Star Belgrade

4. Who scored Liverpool's only goal in the final group game?
(a) Firmino   (b) Sadio Mane   (c) Mohamed Salah

5. Who were the opponents?
(a) Paris Saint-Germain   (b) Napoli   (c) Red Star Belgrade

6.Who finished top of Liverpool's group?
(a) Paris Saint-Germain   (b) Napoli   (c) Red Star Belgrade

7. Who scored twice in Munich in the round of 16?
(a) Joel Matip   (b) Sadio Mane   (c) Fabinho

8. What was the aggregate score in the round of 16?
(a) 2-1   (b) 3-1   (c) 3-2

9. Who were Liverpool's quarter-final opponents?
(a) Ajax   (b) Benfica   (c) Porto

10. Who scored Liverpool's opening goal of the tie?
(a) Naby Keita   (b) Georginio Wijnaldum   (c) Fabinho

11. Who scored the opening goal in the second leg?
(a) Mohamed Salah   (b) Virgil van Dijk   (c) Sadio Mane

12. What was the aggregate score?
(a) 4-1   (b) 5-1   (c) 6-1

13. How many goals did Messi score in the semi-final first leg at the Nou Camp?
(a) one   (b) two   (c) three

14. Who scored Liverpool's first goal in the second leg?
(a) Divock Origi   (b) Georginio Wijnaldum   (c) Firmino

15. Who took the quick corner that led to Liverpool's fourth goal?
(a) Xherdan Shaqiri   (b) Divock Origi   (c) Trent Alexander-Arnold

16. How much time had been played?
(a) 74mins   (b) 79mins   (c) 84mins

17. In which stadium was the final played?
(a) Santiago Bernabeu   (b) La Cartuja   (c) Metropolitano

18. Which Tottenham player conceded a penalty with a handball?
(a) Toby Alderweireld   (b) Moussa Sissoko   (c) Danny Rose

19. How much time had been played?
(a) 22secs   (b) 33secs   (c) 44secs

20. Who scored Liverpool's second goal?
(a) Roberto Firmino   (b) Xherdan Shaqiri   (c) Divock Origi

(Answers p185)

Bob Paisley

1. In which county was Bob Paisley born?
(a) South Yorkshire   (b) Lancashire   (c) Durham

2. What year was he born?
(a) 1914   (b) 1919   (c) 1924

3. Which club did he first join but never play a first-team game for?
(a) Blyth Spartans   (b) Colchester   (c) Bishop Auckland

4. Which branch of the armed forces did he serve with in the Second World War?
(a) Army   (b) Navy   (c) Air Force

5. What year did he sign for Liverpool?
(a) 1929   (b) 1939   (c) 1949

6. How many games did he play for Liverpool?
(a) 53   (b) 153   (c) 253

7. What position did he play?
(a) left-half   (b) left-back   (c) inside forward

8. How many years did he serve as Liverpool captain?
(a) three   (b) five   (c) seven

9. What back room job did he take at Anfield after retiring from playing in
(a) trainer   (b) kit man   (c) physiotherapist

10. What year did he become Liverpool manager?
(a) 1972   (b) 1974   (c) 1976

11. How many League titles did he win at Liverpool?
(a) four   (b) five   (c) six

12. How many FA Cups did he win at Liverpool?
(a) none   (b) one   (c) two

13. How many times was he named Manager of the Year?
(a) two   (b) four   (c) six

14. How many European Cups did he win at Liverpool?
a) two   (b) three   (c) four

15. What honour was he awarded in 1983?
(a) MBE   (b) OBE   (c) CBE

(Answers p186)

Name the Ten...

...Goalkeepers who have worn Liverpool's number one shirt in the Premier League

1 _____ (1993-94)

2 _____ (1994-99)

3 _____ (1999-2001)

4 _____ (2002-07)

5 _____ (2008-10)

6 _____ (2010-15),

7 _____ 2016-18)

8 _____ (2019-)

9 _____ (2020-)

10 _____ (2020-)

(Answers p186)

How Tall? (part 4)

	Player	Years at club	Height
1	Michael Owen	1996–2004	
2	Danny Murphy	1997–2004	
3	Steven Gerrard	1998–2015	
4	Stephane Henchoz	1999–2005	
5	Sami Hyypia	1999–2009	
6	Dietmar Hamann	1999–2006	
7	Vladimír Smicer	1999–2005	
8	Djimi Traore	1999–2006	
9	Markus Babbel	2000–2004	
10	Gary McAllister	2000–2002	
11	Emile Heskey	2000–2004	
12	Jerzy Dudek	2001–2007	
13	John Arne Riise	2001–2008	
14	Milan Baros	2002–2005	
15	Harry Kewell	2003–2008	
16	Luis García	2004–2007	
17	Xabi Alonso	2004–2009	
18	Djibril Cissé	2004–2007	
19	Pepe Reina	2005–2014	
20	Daniel Agger	2006–2014	

Score half a point if you're an inch out either way. Half inches are rounded up.

(Answers p187)

Kenny Dalglish

1. What year was Kenny born?
(a) 1941   (b) 1946   (c) 1951

2. Which team did he support as a child?
(a) Celtic   (b) Rangers   (c) Aberdeen

3. Which club did he play for from 1969 to 1977?
(a) Celtic   (b) Rangers   (c) Aberdeen

4. How many appearances did he make for Liverpool?
(a) 402   (b) 502   (c) 602

5. How many goals did he score for Liverpool?
(a) 169   (b) 199   (c) 229

6. In what year did he win both the Ballon d'Or Silver and the PFA Players' Player of the Year Award?
(a) 1979   (b) 1981   (c) 1983

7. How many full Scotland caps did he earn?
(a) 62   (b) 82   (c) 102

8. In what year did he become Liverpool's player-manager?
(a) 1985   (b) 1986   (c) 1987

9. Which club did he manage from 1997 to 1998?
(a) Blackburn Rovers   (b) Newcastle United   (c) Aston Villa

10. How many League titles did he win with Liverpool as a player and manager?
(a) six   (b) seven   (c) eight

11. How many FA Cups did he win as a player (excluding player-manager)?
(a) none   (b) one   (c) two

12. In what season did he win the League title as Blackburn manager?
(a) 1992-93   (b) 1993-94   (c) 1994–95

13. How many European Cups did he win at Liverpool?
(a) two   (b) three   (c) four

14. How many European Cup final goals did he score?
(a) one   (b) two   (c) three

15. What honour was he awarded in 2018?
(a) OBE   (b) CBE   (c) Knight Bachelor

(Answers p187)

Shoot-outs 8

2016 League Cup Semi-final 2nd leg
Anfield, Tue 26 Jan
Liverpool   0 - 1 **Stoke** (agg: 1-1)

Line-up: Simon Mignolet, Kolo Toure, Mamadou Sakho, Alberto Moreno, Jon Flanagan, James Milner, Jordan Henderson (capt), Adam Lallana, Lucas Leiva, Emre Can, Roberto Firmino
Subs: Christian Benteke, Joe Allen, Jordon Ibe

Fill in in the names of Liverpool's penalty takers below

	Liverpool			Stoke	
			0 - 1	Jon Walters	Scored
1		Scored	1 - 1		
			1 - 1	Peter Crouch	Saved
2		Missed	1 - 1		
			1 - 2	Glenn Whelan	Scored
3		Scored	2 - 2		
			2 - 3	Ibrahim Afellay	Scored
4		Scored	3 - 3		
			3 - 4	Xherdan Shaqiri	Scored
5		Scored	4 - 4		
			4 - 5	Marco van Ginkel	Scored
6		Scored	5 - 5		
			5 - 5	Marc Muniesa	Saved
7		Scored	6 - 5		

(Answers p188)

115

Name the season 4

1. Robbie Fowler makes his debut in September. Manager Graeme Souness resigns in January. The Kop is demolished at the end of the season

2. A new manager takes charge for the start of the season. Liverpool have a 6-0 and two 5-0 home wins in the League. Two Ian Rush goals help secure the FA Cup.

3. Jamie Carragher scores the winning penalty in the shoot-out vs Birmingham to secure the League Cup. A Gary McAllister penalty puts Liverpool through to a European final.

4. Jamie Carragher announces his retirement. A day later Liverpool score four goals in the opening 20 minutes against Arsenal. The 5-1 victory is the start of an 11-game winning streak. Liverpool end the season on 101 league goals; the most scored by a Premier League runner-up.

5. New signing John Toshack scores in his first Merseyside derby to help secure a 3-1 victory. Kevin Keegan is signed from Scunthorpe for £35,000 days after the FA Cup final.

6. Liverpool are top of the League by five points at Christmas but things get "Spicy" in the second half of the season. Liverpool finish fourth, despite being level on points with second place.

7. Wes Brown scores an own goal and Nemanja Vidic is sent off in a 2-1 win over Man United at Anfield. Dirk Kuyt scores a 90th minute winner as Liverpool come from 2-0 down to win 3-2 at the City of Manchester Stadium. Steven

Gerrard is arrested over an incident in a bar, but is cleared of the charges in July.

8. A new manager takes charge at the start of the season. Rush scores five in a 6-0 League win at Anfield. Liverpool win a treble.

9. Luis Suarez leaves for Barcelona before the start of the season. Steven Gerrard departs for LA after the season ends.

10. Liverpool win the League but lose two semi-finals. David Johnson finishes top scorer with 27 goals.

11. Goals from Gerrard and Owen secure the League Cup at the Millenium Stadium. The season ends with two 2-1 defeats, leaving Liverpool in fifth place in the Premier League.

(Answers p188)

Transfers: The 2010s

Match the following clubs to the Liverpool signings

1899 Hoffenheim	Hull	Roma
Ajax	Inter Milan	Southampton
Aston Villa	Lille	Southampton
Atletico Madrid	Newcastle	Sunderland
Bayer Leverkusen	Paris St Germain	Swansea
Blackpool	Red Bull Leipzig	Wycombe
Charlton	Roma	

	Date	Player	Fee	Signed from
1	Jan 2010	Maxi Rodriguez	Free	
2	Jan 2011	Luis Suarez	£22,800,000	
3	Jun 2011	Jordan Henderson	£16,000,000	
4	Jul 2011	Charlie Adam	£6,750,000	
5	Dec 2011	Jordon Ibe	£500,000	
6	Aug 2012	Joe Allen	£15,000,000	
7	Jan 2013	Philippe Coutinho	£8,500,000	
8	Sep 2013	Mamadou Sakho	£15,000,000	
9	Jul 2014	Emre Can	£9,750,000	
10	Jul 2014	Divock Origi	£9,800,000	
11	Jun 2015	Joe Gomez	£6,000,000	
12	Jul 2015	Roberto Firmino	£29,000,000	
13	Jul 2015	Christian Benteke	£32,500,000	
14	Jun 2016	Sadio Mane	£30,000,000	
15	Jul 2016	Georginio Wijnaldum	£25,000,000	
16	Jun 2017	Mohamed Salah	£43,900,000	
17	Jul 2017	Andy Robertson	£10,000,000	
18	Jan 2018	Virgil Van Dijk	£75,000,000	
19	Jul 2018	Naby Keita	£52,750,000	
20	Jul 2018	Alisson Becker	£65,000,000	

Select the clubs that players moved to from Liverpool

Barcelona	Cardiff	Southampton
Barcelona	Chelsea	Stoke
Barcelona	Club Brugge	Stoke
Bayern Munich	Crystal Palace	Sunderland
Bolton	Fenerbahce	Swansea
Bournemouth	Fenerbahce	West Ham
Brondby	Newell's Old Boys	

	Date	Player	Fee	Went to
1	Aug 2010	Javier Mascherano	£17,250,000	
2	Jan 2011	Fernando Torres	£50,000,000	
3	Aug 2011	David N'Gog	£4,000,000	
4	Jun 2012	Dirk Kuyt	£1,000,000	
5	Jul 2012	Maxi Rodriguez	Undisc.	
6	Aug 2012	Craig Bellamy	Undisc.	
7	Aug 2012	Charlie Adam	£5,000,000	
8	Jul 2013	Jonjo Shelvey	£6,000,000	
9	Aug 2013	Stewart Downing	£6,000,000	
10	Jul 2014	Luis Suarez	£65,000,000	
11	Aug 2014	Pepe Reina	£2,000,000	
12	Aug 2014	Daniel Agger	£3,000,000	
13	Aug 2015	Fabio Borini	£10,000,000	
14	Jul 2016	Martin Skrtel	£5,500,000	
15	Jul 2016	Jordon Ibe	£15,000,000	
16	Jul 2016	Joe Allen	£13,000,000	
17	Aug 2017	Mamadou Sakho	£26,000,000	
18	Jan 2018	Philippe Coutinho	£142,000,000	
19	Jul 2019	Danny Ings	£20,000,000	
20	Aug 2019	Simon Mignolet	£8,200,000	

(Answers p189)

119

Kevin Keegan 2

1. What was the injury that kept Keegan out of most of the 1982 World Cup Finals in Spain?
(a) back   (b) groin   (c) knee

2. Where did he finish his playing career in England?
(a) Southampton   (b) Fulham   (c) Newcastle

3. How many times has he won the Ballon d'Or?
(a) none   (b) one   (c) two

4. In what season was he named the PFA Players' Player of the Year?
(a) 1973-74   (b) 1976-77   (c) 1981–82

5. In what season did he lead Newcastle to second place in the Premier League?
(a) 1994-95   (b) 1995–96   (c) 1996-97

6. Which club did he manage from May 1998 to May 1999?
(a) Southampton   (b) Fulham   (c) Brighton

7. Which brand of cereal did he advertise in the 1990s?
(a) Sugar Puffs   (b) Coco Pops   (c) Weetabix

8. Which club did he manage from 2000 to 2005?
(a) Fulham   (b) Southampton   (c) Manchester City

9. How many Uefa Cups did he win with Liverpool?
(a) none   (b) one   (c) two

10. In what year did he first play for England?
(a) 1972   (b) 1973   (c) 1974

11. How many European Cup finals did he play in?
(a) one   (b) two   (c) three

12. How tall is he?
(a) 5ft 6   (b) 5ft 7   (c) 5ft 8

13. What honour was he awarded in 1982?
(a) MBE   (b) OBE   (c) CBE

14. How many times has he scored in an FA Cup final?
(a) two   (b) three   (c) four

15. How many League titles did he win with Liverpool?
(a) two   (b) three   (c) four

(Answers p190)

Who Said That? (part 4)

1. "Liverpool was made for me and I was made for Liverpool."
(a) Kevin Keegan   (b) Steven Gerrard   (c) Bill Shankly

2. "Winning trophies has made me put on weight."
(a) Rafa Benitez   (b) Bob Paisley   (c) Kenny Dalglish

3. "I had fourth-division feet and a first-division head."
(a) Kevin Keegan   (b) Tommy Smith   (c) Jurgen Klopp

4. "When they start singing 'You'll Never Walk Alone' my eyes start to water. There have been times when I've actually been crying while I've been playing."
(a) Emlyn Hughes   (b) Kevin Keegan   (c) Jamie Carragher

5. "If Shankly was the Anfield foreman, Paisley was the brickie, ready to build an empire with his own hands."
(a) Tommy Smith (b) Graeme Souness   (c) Kenny Dalglish

6. "There's no noise like the Anfield noise."
(a) Bill Shankly   (b) Robbie Fowler   (c) Ian St John

7. "We murdered them 0-0."
(a) Kevin Keegan   (b) Bill Shankly (c) Gerard Houllier

8. "At a football club, there's a holy trinity - the players, the manager and the supporters. Directors don't come into it. They are only there to sign the cheques."
(a) Bill Shankly   (b) Kenny Dalglish   (c) John Henry

9. "It's forever. It's not just about a football club, it's about family, how you live."
(a) Jamie Carragher   (b) Bob Paisley   (c) Xabi Alonso

10. "I said that when I took over that I would settle for a drop of Bell's once a month, a big bottle at the end of the season and a ride round the city in an open top bus."
(a) Bob Paisley   (b) Bill Shankly   (c) Rafa Benitez

(Answers p191)

Liverpool Facts

Since the establishment of the club in 1892, 45 players have been club captain of Liverpool Alex Raisbeck, who was captain from 1899 to 1909, was the longest serving before being overtaken by Steven Gerrard, who served 12 seasons as Liverpool captain starting from the 2003–04 season..

Anagrams: Liverpool Managers

Rearrange the letters to form the names of Liverpool managers. (NB: It is strictly prohibited to look at the list of managers on pages 134 & 135 and then work your way backwards. I repeat…)

(1) Handles kingly   _ _ _ _ _ / _ _ _ _ _ _ _ _

(2) Brazen lie feat   _ _ _ _ _ _ / _ _ _ _ _ _ _

(3) Enrages mouses   _ _ _ _ _ _ _ / _ _ _ _ _ _ _

(4) Hilly blanks   _ _ _ / _ _ _ _ _ _ _

(5) Ron badgers nerd   _ _ _ _ _ _ _ _ / _ _ _ _ _ _ _ _

(6) Horny goods   _ _ _ / _ _ _ _ _ _ _

(7) Guerrilla horde   _ _ _ _ _ _ _ / _ _ _ _ _ _ _ _

(8) Navy rose   _ _ _ / _ _ _ _ _

(9) Soapy bible   _ _ _ / _ _ _ _ _ _ _

(10) Greek yoga   _ _ _ _ _ / _ _ _ _

(Answers p191)

Shoot-outs 9

2019 European Super Cup
Beşiktass Park, Wed 14 Aug
Liverpool   2 - 2 **Chelsea**

Line-up: Adrian San Miguel, Virgil Van Dijk, Joe Gomez, Andy Robertson, Joel Matip, Fabinho Tavarez, James Milner, Jordan Henderson (capt), Alex Oxlade-Chamberlain, Sadio Mane, Mohamed Salah
Subs: Roberto Firmino, Georginio Wijnaldum, Trent Alexander-Arnold, Divock Origi

Fill in Liverpool's penalty takers below

	Liverpool			Chelsea	
1		Scored	1 - 0		
			1 - 1	Jorginho	scored
2		scored	2 - 1		
			2 - 2	Ross Barkley	scored
3		scored	3 - 2		
			3 - 3	Mason Mount	scored
4		scored	4 - 3		
			4 - 4	Emerson Palmieri	scored
5		scored	5 - 4		
			5 - 4	Tammy Abraham	saved

(Answers p191)

Graeme Souness

1. Where was Graeme Souness born?
(a) Edinburgh   (b) Glasgow   (c) Dundee

2. What year was he born?
(a) 1950   (b) 1953   (c) 1956

3. Which club did he sign for as a 15-year old but only make one appearance?
(a) Sunderland   (b) Newcastle   (c) Tottenham

4. Which club did Liverpool sign him from in January 1978?
(a) Rangers   (b) Middlesbrough   (c) Sunderland

5. What fee did Liverpool pay?
(a) £350,000   (b) £450,000   (c) £550,000

6. How many appearances did he make for Liverpool?
(a) 258   (b) 358   (c) 458

7. How many goals did he score for Liverpool?
(a) 56   (b) 66   (c) 76

8. In which 1982 BBC drama did he appear?
(a) The Borgias   (b) The Monocled Mutineer   (c) Boys from the Blackstuff

9. Which Italian club did he join after leaving Liverpool in 1984?
(a) Torino   (b) Sampdoria   (c) Juventus

10. What fee did Liverpool receive for him?
(a) £550,000   (b) £650,000   (c) £750,000

11. At which club did he become player-manager in 1986?
(a) Middlesbrough   (b) Southampton   (c) Rangers

12. In what year did he become Liverpool manager?
(a) 1991   (b) 1992   (c) 1993

13. Who did he sign for an English record fee of £2.9m in July 1991?
(a) Peter Beardsley   (b) Mark Wright   (c) Dean Saunders

14. At whose hands did his Liverpool side suffer a shock FA Cup exit in January 1994?
(a) Port Vale   (b) Colchester   (c) Bristol City

15. How many League titles did he win at Liverpool?
(a) four   (b) five   (c) six

(Answers p192)

Name the Eleven...

... Liverpool players who started the 1984 European Cup final

Match the players to the shirt number they wore that day

1 _____

2 _____

3 _____

4 _____

5 _____

6 _____

7 _____

8 _____

9 _____

10 _____

11 _____

... Liverpool players who started the 2005 Champions League Final

Match the players to the shirt number they wore that day

1 _____

3 _____

23 _____

4 _____

21 _____

14 _____

10 _____

8 _____

6 _____

7 _____

5 _____

... Liverpool players who started the 2019 Champions League Final

Match the players to the shirt number they wore that day

13 _____

66 _____

32 _____

4 _____

26 _____

14 _____

3 _____

5 _____

11 _____

9 _____

10 _____

(Answers p192)

Where are they from? (part 4)

Fill in the players' countries of birth below

	Player	Years at club	Country of birth
1	Daniel Agger	2006–14	
2	Javier Mascherano	2007–10	
3	Yossi Benayoun	2007–10	
4	Ryan Babel	2007–11	
5	Fernando Torres	2007–11	
6	Lucas Leiva	2007–17	
7	Albert Riera	2008–10	
8	David N'Gog	2008–11	
9	Martin Škrtel	2008–16	
10	Maxi Rodríguez	2010–12	
11	Brad Jones	2010–15	
12	Luis Suárez	2011–14	
13	José Enrique	2011–16	
14	Fabio Borini	2012–15	
15	Kolo Toure	2013–16	
16	Mamadou Sakho	2013–17	
17	Philippe Coutinho	2013–18	
18	Simon Mignolet	2013–19	
19	Emre Can	2014–18	
20	Christian Benteke	2015–16	

(Answers p193)

A Quiz That's Lacking in Options

1. Who is the second highest scoring Welshman for Liverpool behind Ian Rush?

_____

2. In which season did Liverpool adopt an all-red home kit?

_____

3. Who wore the No.8 jersey at Liverpool before Steven Gerrard?

_____

4. Who are the only team Liverpool have scored seven against in one game in the Premier League?

_____

5. Name two English stadiums Liverpool have played in during the Premier League era beginning with the letter 'F'?

_____

6. Who was Kenny Dalglish's last signing during his first spell as Liverpool manager?

_____

7. Who was the last player to be directly transferred between Liverpool and Man United?

_____

8. Who are the only club Liverpool have failed to beat in the Premier League?

_____

9. Which away ground that Liverpool have played at in the Premier League comes first alphabetically?

_____

10. Which former Liverpool manager has a brown belt in judo?

_____

(Answers p194)

133

Liverpool Statistics

Managers (1892-1983)

Name	From	To	Win %	L	FA	LC	EC / CL	UC	Tot
William Barclay John McKenna	Feb 1892	Aug 1896	60.6						
Tom Watson	Aug 1896	May 1915	44.3	2					2
David Ashworth	Oct 1919	Feb 1923	50.4	1					1
Matt McQueen	Feb 1923	Feb 1928	40.6	1					1
George Patterson	Mar 1928	Aug 1936	37.4						
George Kay	Aug 1936	Jan 1951	39.8	1					1
Don Welsh	Mar 1951	May 1956	34.9						
Phil Taylor	May 1956	Nov 1959	50.7						
Bill Shankly	Dec 1959	Jul 1974	52.0	3	2			1	6
Bob Paisley	Aug 1974	Jul 1983	57.6	6		3	3	1	13

L = League; FA = FA Cup; LC = League Cup; EC / CL=
European Cup / Champions League; UC = Uefa Cup
European competitions only

Managers (1983 – present)

Name	From	To	Win %	L	FA	LC	EC / CL	UC	Tot
					Major Trophies				
Joe Fagan	Jul 1983	May 1985	54.2	1		1	1		3
Kenny Dalglish	May 1985	Feb 1991	60.9	3	2				5
Ronnie Moran	Feb 1991	Apr 1991	40.0						
Graeme Souness	Apr 1991	Jan 1994	42.0		1				1
Roy Evans	Jan 1994	Nov 1998	51.8			1			1
Roy Evans Gerard Houllier	Jul 1998	Nov 1998	38.9						
Gerard Houllier	Jul 1998	May 2004	52.1		1	2		1	4
Rafael Benítez	Jun 2004	Jun 2010	55.4		1		1		2
Roy Hodgson	Jul 2010	Jan 2011	41.9						
Kenny Dalglish	Jan 2011	May 2012	47.3			1			1
Brendan Rodgers	Jun 2012	Oct 2015	50.0						
Jurgen Klopp	Oct 2015	*pres*	61.0	1			1		2

L = League; FA = FA Cup; LC = League Cup; EC / CL= European Cup / Champions League; UC = Uefa Cup European competitions only

All-time Top Goalscorers

	Name	Years	Lge	FA	Gl	Ga	GPG
1	Ian Rush	1980–87 1988–96	229 (469)	39 (61)	346	660	0.52
2	Roger Hunt	1958–69	244 (404)	18 (44)	285	492	0.58
3	Gordon Hodgson	1925–36	233 (358)	8 (19)	241	377	0.64
4	Billy Liddell	1938–61	215 (492)	13 (42)	228	534	0.43
5	Steven Gerrard	1998–15	120 (503)	15 (40)	186	710	0.36
6	Robbie Fowler	1993–01 2006–07	128 (266)	12 (24)	183	369	0.50
7	Kenny Dalglish	1977–90	118 (355)	13 (37)	172	515	0.33
8	Michael Owen	1996–04	118 (216)	8 (15)	158	297	0.53
9	Harry Chambers	1915–28	135 (315)	16 (28)	151	339	0.45
10	Sam Raybould	1900–07	120 (211)	9 (14)	130	226	0.58

FA = FA Cup; Gl= goals; Ga = games; GPG = goals per game
Appearances in brackets

All-time Goals Per Game

	Player	Date	Goals	Games	GPG
1	Jimmy Stott	1893-94	14	17	0.824
2	Willie Devlin	1927	15	19	0.789
3	Fred Pagnam	1914-19	30	39	0.769
4	Gordon Hodgson	1925–36	241	377	0.639
5	Mohamed Salah	2017–	115	183	0.628
6	Luis Suarez	2011-14	82	133	0.616
7	Jimmy Smith	1929-31	38	62	0.613
8	John Aldridge	1987-89	63	104	0.606
9	Tony Rowley	1954-58	38	63	0.603
10	George Allan	1895-99	56	96	0.583
11	Jack Parkinson	1903–14	128	219	0.584
12	Roger Hunt	1958–69	285	492	0.579
13	Sam Raybould	1900–07	130	226	0.575
14	Fernando Torres	2007-11	81	142	0.570
15	Dave Hickson	1959-61	38	67	0.567
16	Tom Reid	1926-29	30	55	0.545
17	Kevin Lewis	1960-63	44	82	0.536
18	Michael Owen	1996–04	158	297	0.532
19	Ian Rush	1980–87 1988–96	346	660	0.524
20	David Henderson	1893-94	12	23	0.522

Most consecutive games

Player	Games	From	To
Phil Neal	417	23 Oct 1976	24 Sep 1983
Ray Clemence	336	9 Sep 1972	4 May 1978
Bruce Grobbelaar	317	29 Aug 1981	16 Aug 1986
Chris Lawler	316	2 Oct 1965	24 Apr 1971
David James	213	19Feb 1994	23 Feb 1998
Alan Kennedy	205	23 Jan 1982	31 Mar 1985
Ian Callaghan	185	17 Aug 1971	7 Sep 1974
Kenny Dalglish	180	13 Aug 1977	23 Aug 1980
Emlyn Hughes	177	31 Oct 1972	25 Oct 1975
Peter Thompson	153	1 Sep1965	13 Apr 1968

The Greatest Comebacks

Date	Opponents	Deficit	Competition	Result
4 Dec 1909	Newcastle (h)	2-5 at half-time	First Division	Won 6-5
21 Nov 1970	Everton (h)	0-2 after 68mins	First Division	Won 3-2
29 Sep 1992	Chesterfield (h)	0-3 after 48mins	Lge Cup R2	4-4
4 Jan 1994	Man United (h)	0-3 after 24mins	Prem League	3-3
25 May 2005	Inter Milan	0-3 at half-time	Champions League final	3-3 (W3-2 pens)
13 May 2006	West Ham	0-2 after 28mins	FA Cup final	3-3 (W3-1 pens)

All-time Trophies Ranking

	Lge	FAC	LC	EC CL	UC	CWC	FC	Total
Liverpool	19	7	8	6	3			43
Man United	20	12	5	3	1	1		42
Arsenal	13	14	2			1	1	31
Chelsea	6	8	5	1	2	2		24
Aston Villa	7	7	5	1				20
Man City	6	6	7			1		20
Tottenham	2	8	4		2	1		17
Everton	9	5				1		15
Newcastle	4	6					1	11
Blackburn	3	6	1					10
Notts Forest	1	2	4	2				9
Wolves	3	4	2					9
Sheff Wed	4	3	1					8
Sunderland	6	2						8
West Brom	1	5	1					7
Leeds	3	1	1				2	7
Sheff United	1	4						5
Leicester	1		3					4
Portsmouth	2	2						4
Bolton		4						4

Lge = League; FAC = FA Cup; LC = League Cup; EC / CL =
European Cup / Champions Lge; CWC = Cup Winners'Cup,;
FC = Fairs Cup. European competitions only

Appearances

	Player	Years	Lge	FA	LC	Other	Total
1	Ian Callaghan	1960–78	640	79	42	96	**857**
2	Jamie Carragher	1996–13	508	40	35	152	**737**
3	Steven Gerrard	1998–15	504	42	30	134	**710**
4	Ray Clemence	1967–81	470	54	55	86	**665**
	Emlyn Hughes	1967–79	474	62	46	83	**665**
6	Ian Rush	1980–87 1988–96	469	61	78	45	**660**
7	Phil Neal	1974–85	455	45	66	81	**650**
8	Tommy Smith	1962–78	467	52	30	89	**638**
9	Bruce Grobbelaar	1980–94	440	62	70	46	**628**
10	Alan Hansen	1977–91	434	58	68	53	**620**

Competitive matches only

Top flight points

		P	W	D	L	GD	Pts
1	**Liverpool**	4191	1977	1041	1173	1933	6972
2	**Arsenal**	4191	1908	1074	1209	1687	6798
3	**Everton**	4573	1860	1147	1566	767	6727
4	**Man United**	3835	1840	944	1051	1749	6464
5	**Aston Villa**	4124	1660	978	1486	516	5958
6	**Man City**	3676	1489	881	1306	559	5348
7	**Tottenham**	3450	1435	837	1178	642	5142
8	**Chelsea**	3455	1414	887	1154	478	5129
9	**Newcastle**	3520	1353	855	1312	163	4914
10	**Sunderland**	3340	1260	780	1300	22	4560
11	**West Brom**	3127	1102	770	1255	-339	4076
12	**Blackburn**	2720	1017	651	1052	-42	3702
13	**Bolton**	2802	1017	641	1144	-311	3692
14	**Sheff Wed**	2582	980	612	990	-44	3552
15	**Wolves**	2517	980	573	964	82	3513
16	**Derby**	2468	906	585	977	-146	3303
17	**Sheff Utd**	2413	886	574	953	-253	3232
18	**West Ham**	2529	858	630	1041	-400	3204
19	**Leeds**	2078	853	525	700	291	3084
20	**Burnley**	2228	855	504	869	-120	3069

Figures correct as of Feb 2021

Liverpool History

The Liver Bird

The origins of the Liverpool's legendary bird probably date to 1229, when Henry III granted the borough (which had been founded 22 years earlier by King John) the right to form a guild and use a common seal.

Although the earliest surviving impression of the seal, from 1352, features a dove-like bird, it's believed that a goose, long-necked heron and possibly an eagle may have been used at different times. The sprig in the bird's mouth is most likely to have been the broom plant, a symbol of the Plantagenets who ruled the country.

By 1611 the bird on the "Townes Armes" was recorded as a cormorant. We don't know whether this was the official description as the city was captured by Prince Rupert during the Civil War in 1644 and "all the wrytings and ancient records belonging to ye said Corporation were taken away".

The city soon commissioned "one new Seal ingraved with the Townes' arms", though the 1688 *Academie of Armorie*, records it containing a "lever", most likely an adaptation of the German "Loffler" or Dutch "lepler", meaning a spoonbill (a bird with longer legs and beak than a cormorant).

It is possible that these continental words were adopted for the bird in Liverpool's arms as they alluded to the name "Liverpool". Around this time the broom sprig in the bird's beak was reinterpreted as a branch of laver seaweed, also on account of the similarity of the word to the city's name..

In 1796 the Mayor of Liverpool wrote to the College of Arms to request an official grant of arms, which he described as containing "a lever or sea cormorant". The following year the College settled the matter, declaring the bird to be a cormorant, and having "a. branch of seaweed called Laver" in its beak – a depiction that has continued to the present day.

So why a cormorant? It might be they were present in the area during the Middle Ages (unfortunately, bird spotters weren't common back then). It's also likely they were regarded as symbols of sea power. Or it could just be the adoption of the cormorant allowed the engraver to convert the original sprig of foliage into a sprig of edible seaweed, the cormorant's natural food.

Although the liver bird features in engravings on a number of Liverpool buildings in the19th century, it wasn't until 1911 that it became associated with the city in popular culture. The reason was the opening of the Liver Building, the headquarters of the Royal Livers Friendly Society. The giant copper birds—each. around 18ft high with wing-spans of 24ft—on top of its two clock towers were soon dubbed the the "Liver Birds". They were designed to keep watch over the city's people and its prosperity. The male, Bertie, looks over the city while the female, Bella looks to the sea.

The city's emblem had been associated with Liverpool Football Club since its formation. In September 1892, following a home match against Bury, *The National Field* newspaper described "a flag floated on the old staff, bearing the letters L.F.C surmounted with the Liver. Right proudly did it wave over the field of battle and seemed to beam on its patrons with a hopeful smile."

The club initially took city's coat of arms as its emblem, which features the Roman god of freshwater and the sea, Neptune, and the Greek god and messenger of the sea, Triton, flanking two cormorants. But after Liverpool won their third League title in 1922, a new banner was introduced that featured the Liver bird more prominently.

By the late 1940s the club had an alternative crest featuring a single Liver bird with a football either side, that was used on letterheads and match-day programmes. The Liver bird crest first appeared on the club's white shirts in the 1950 FA Cup final, featuring a white bird on a red shield.

The crest was revived for the 1955-56 season, but now featured a red Liver bird in a white oval with LFC embroidered below it. The Liver bird has featured on the shirt ever since, sometimes in white and at other times in gold.

So which is the luckiest colour of bird?

Liver bird	Years worn	Seas-ons	Lge	EC / CL	UC	FAC	LC	Total
White	1968-76 & 1985-92	14	5		2	4		11
Red	1955-68 & 1992-12	33	2	1	1	3	4	11
Gold	1976-85 & 2012-	17	7	5			4	16

The History of Liverpool's Kit

Liverpool's earliest kit was Cambridge blue and white halves with dark blue shorts and socks. As these were the same colours that Everton wore between 1887 to 1890 it's likely that they had left them behind after vacating Anfield in March 1892 (Everton were at that time playing in ruby red shirts and dark blue shorts).

On 1 September 1896 Liverpool wore red for the first time. The reason for the switch is unclear. As red is the municipal colour of Liverpool it's possible they wanted to identify more with city, though they may have just wanted to distinguish themselves more from their near neighbours, who had also been wearing Cambridge blue shirts since late 1892. According to a newspaper report the new kit had, "a dark red or black stand collar with buttons down the front and white pants," though a team photograph from that season shows them in black shorts.

In 1902 the buttoned collar was replaced with a high drawstring, with heavy, ribbed wool now being used instead of traditional shirt material. But a red shirt and white shorts remained the teams colours until 1965. For most of that time the socks were red, though black with a red hoop turnover was worn from 1907 to 1910, while black socks with a solid red turnover were worn in 1931-32 and 1934-1936. In 1936 red and white hooped socks were introduced, before being replaced by white with a red turnover in 1959.

Red shorts were first worn in a European match against Anderlecht in the 1964-65 season. According to Ian St John's autobiography, "*He* (Shankly) *thought the colour scheme would carry psychological impact—red for danger,*

*red for power. He came into the dressing room one day and
threw a pair of red shorts to Ronnie Yeats. "Get into those
shorts and let's see how you look," he said. "Christ,
Ronnie, you look awesome, terrifying. You look 7ft tall."*

Initially Liverpool wore their regular white socks but on 3
February 1965, all-red socks were introduced in an FA
fourth round replay against Stockport, at the suggestion of
St John. Initially only worn in FA Cup and European
matches, after winning the FA Cup in May the iconic all-
red strip became Liverpool's first choice colours—and have
been ever since.

How the City got its Name

The "-pool" part of the city's name originates from the Old English word "pol", an estuary of a small stream as it widens into the sea. "Liver-" might be derived from the Old English word 'Lifrig', meaning 'coagulated' or, 'clotted'. Alternatively it may be the old name of one of the streams that fed into the pol.

The earliest known spelling of the city's name, from 1190-94, is Liuerpul, but it was also spelt Liuerpol (1211, 1246 and 1266); Litherpol (1222-26); Leuerepul (1229); Lyuerpole (1346), Leuerpoll (1393) and Lyuerpull (1458). The city was first referred to as "Liverpool" in the following sentence from a 1540 guide book: "Good merchandise at Liverpool and much Irish yarn, that Manchester men buy there."

Legal documents from 1548 and 1557, though, refer to the Mayor of "Lyverpole", and it wasn't until the creation of newspapers in the late 1700s that spellings became standardized.

By the early 19th century there was only one Liverpool, though the first 'Liverpudlian' did not appear until 1833.

When Liverpool Tried to Banish the Blues

Did you know that a Liverpool chairman once tried to ban teams from wearing blue in League matches?

In 1906 new Liverpool chairman John McKenna put forward the following bold proposal during a meeting of the Football League:

Rule 15: Delete this rule and substitute—
The playing colours of the League shall be red shirts or jerseys and white knickers and white shirts or jerseys and dark knickers. The annual general meeting shall decide which are to be the home colours.

McKenna argued "that many of the club's colours were conflicting and bothersome to referees." Man United's representative Earnest Magnall seconded the motion though, unsurprisingly, representatives from teams who played in blue were not exactly happy.

Blackburn Rovers' Mr Middleton "pointed out that there were sentimental objections to the course, and they ought to consider the feelings of supporters", while Birmingham City's Mr Hart thought the proposal would lead to endless confusion among the clubs.

The motion was lost.

Forgotten Goal Machines:

John Miller (1892-93)

The leading goalscorer in Dumbarton's 1891-92 Scottish title-winning season, the signing of Miller in June 1892 represented quite a coup for newly-formed Liverpool, who had just joined the Lancashire League.

According to *Field Sports*, Miller was "an ideal centre… feeding his forwards with remarkable accuracy, and when a chance of scoring presents itself his shots are sent with a velocity that gives the goalkeeper little chance."

He scored 25 goals in 24 games in his only season at Anfield, making him the only Liverpool player in history to average more than a goal a game. He also became the first of only five Liverpool players to score five goals in match.

But a player who joins for the money is most likely to leave for the same reason. After Liverpool were admitted into the Football League Second Division, Miller demanded a £100 payment (the equivalent of two years wages for a skilled manual worker) plus a £3 a week for the following season. After the club turned him down he signed for First Division side The Wednesday, which the *Athletic News* concluded "must be paying him a heavy sum."

Fred Pagnam (1914-19)

A £75 signing from Blackpool in 1914, the 22-year-old Pagnam was "generally recognised as the best find of the year in Division One circles," according to the *Liverpool Echo*.

His 26 goals from 31 games that season makes him Liverpool's most deadly striker since joining the Football League. But like so many, his professional career was cut short by the First World War bringing the League to a halt at the end of the 1914-15 season.

He maintained his prolific scoring record for Liverpool in friendly wartime matches, with 43 goals in 49 matches, and was back in the goals when the League resumed in 1919, with four goals in the first eight matches.

But with clubs hard-pressed for funds following four seasons without League and Cup football Pagnam was sold to Arsenal for £1,500, the biggest transfer of that season.

After spells at Cardiff City and Watford, where he famously scored three hat-tricks in five games before becoming their manager, he took charge of the Turkish national team in 1931 before coaching in the Netherlands until the war forced him to escape the Nazis with his Dutch wife in 1940.

Willie Devlin (1927)

The Scottish town of Bellshill has produced more footballing greats—from Sir Matt Busby to Billy McNeill—than any place on earth.

Perhaps most remarkable is that Devlin, who was born in the North Lanarkshire town in 1899 and went on to score 214 career goals in 283 games, isn't even its most prolific striker (Bellshill's Hughie Gallacher scored 463 goals in 624 senior games between 1921-39).

After scoring 77 goals in 68 matches for Cowdenbeath between 1924-1926, Devlin signed for English champions Huddersfield Town for £4,200—a huge fee at the time. The following season he joined Liverpool. There was great excitement at the signing of a player who could shoot on the run with either foot, and after scoring on his debut he went on to net 14 in the next 15, including four goals against both Bury (5-1) and Portsmouth (8-2).

But after picking up an injury, Devlin only played three more games for Liverpool, scoring in none, before being sold to Hearts. A year later he was playing for Macclesfield in the Cheshire League.

But his 15 goals in 19 games during his brief stay at Anfield makes Devlin the club's second most deadly striker ever.

Answers

Answers: The Early Years

1. (a) 15 March 1892
2. (b) John Houlding
3. (c) Anfield Masonic Lodge Littlewoods
4. (a) brewer
5. (a) Lord Mayor of Liverpool
6. (b) blue and white
7. (a) 1894
8. (c) Lancashire League
9. (c) John McKenna
10. (c) the team of Macs
11. (b) Liverpool District Cup
12. (a) 1893
13. (b) Middlesbrough Ironopolis
14. (a) first (Liverpool then beat second-place Newton Heath in a play-off to win promotion)
15. (a) Tom Watson
16. (b) £300 (making Watson the highest-paid manager in England at the time)
17. (b) 1896–97 (they lost 3-0 to Aston Villa)
18. (a) 1900-01
19. (c) Sam Raybould (in 1905 he became the first Liverpool player to score a hat trick against Man United)
20. (b) Alex Raisbeck

Answers: Jamie Carragher

1. (b) Bootle
2. (c) Everton (as a youngster Carragher regularly turned up at Liverpool's School of Excellence wearing a Graeme Sharp Everton kit)
3. (b) 1996-97 (in the League Cup quarter-final at Middlesbrough on 8 January 1997)
4. (c) 23
5. (a) 2002 FIFA World Cup
6. (b) 17
7. (c) 737
8. (c) Álvaro Arbeloa
9. (b) 6ft 1
10. (a) Arsenal
11. (b) two (1998–99 & 2004/05)
12. (a) 5
13. (b) £1million
14. (a) 38
15. (c) Carra: My Autobiography

Answers: The 1976–77 European Cup

1. (b) Northern Ireland
2. (c) 7-0
3. (a) Trabzonspor
4. (b) 19mins
5. (c) Saint-Etienne
6. (b) David Fairclough
7. (a) 84mins
8. (a) Phil Neal
9. (c) 6-1
10. (c) Stadio Olimpico
11. (b) 52,000
12. (a) Tommy Smith

Answers: How Tall? The Current Squad

	Player	Height
1	Alisson	6ft 3
2	Adrian	6ft 3
3	Virgil van Dijk	6ft 4
4	Joe Gomez	6ft 2
5	Andy Robertson	5ft 10
6	Joël Matip	6ft 5
7	Trent Alexander-Arnold	5ft 9
8	Fabinho	6ft 2
9	Georginio Wijnaldum	5ft 9
10	Thiago	5ft 9
11	James Milner	5ft 9
12	Naby Keita	5ft 8
13	Jordan Henderson	6ft 0
14	Alex Oxlade-Chamberlain	5ft 11
15	Curtis Jones	6ft 1
16	Diogo Jota	5ft 10
17	Xherdan Shaqiri	5ft 7
18	Roberto Firmino	5ft 11
19	Sadio Mane	5ft 9
20	Mohamed Salah	5ft 9

Answers: Anagrams

1. Donald McKinlay
2. Jack Balmer
3. Ron Yeats
4. Peter Thompson
5. Ray Clemence
6. John Toshack
7. Phil Neal
8. Sammy Lee
9. Alan Kennedy
10. Mark Lawrenson

Answers: Shoot-outs - 1974 Charity Shield

1	Alec Lindsay
2	Emlyn Hughes
3	Brian Hall
4	Tommy Smith
5	Peter Cormack
6	Ian Callaghan

Answers: Mohamed Salah

1. (c) 1992
2. (a) Egypt
3. (c) 4-4½ hrs
4. (b) Al Mokawloon
5. (a) Basel
6. (c) Chelsea
7. (a) Roma
8. (b) €15 million
9. (c) June 2017
10. (b) £36.5m (rising to £43m)
11. (a) 26
12. (b) four
13. (c) 44 (in 52 appearances)
14. (c) Egyptian King
15. (b) two (in 2017–18 & 2018–19)

Answers: The 1977–78 European Cup

1. (c) Dynamo Dresden
2. (b) 5-1
3. (a) Benfica
4. (c) Emlyn Hughes

5. (c) Borussia Mönchengladbach
6. (a) David Johnson
7. (c) Dusseldorf, (Mönchengladbach's Bökelbergstadion only had a 34,500 capacity)
8. (b) 4-2
9. (a) Club Brugge
10. (c) Wembley Stadium
11. (b) Kenny Dalglish
12. (c) Jimmy Case (with four goals)

Answers: Ian Rush

1. (b) 1961
2. (c) Chester City
3. (a) 18
4. (c) £300,000 (then a record fee for a teenager)
5. (a) 3 minutes (on 30 Sept 1981 vs Oulun Palloseura.in the first round of the European Cup)
6. (b) Tottenham (Rush also scored in both legs of the semi)
7. (c) Juventus
8. (c) £3.2m (then a British transfer record)
9. (b) £2.7m (then a record amount for an English club)
10. (b) 346
11. (c) 73
12. (b) eight (1981–82, 1982–83, 1983–84, 1985–86, 1986–87, 1990–91, 1992–93, 1993–94)
13. (b) Wrexham
14. (a) MBE
15. (a) Chester City

Answers: Name the Three...

... Liverpool players in England's 1966 WC squad
Gerry Byrne, Ian Callaghan and Roger Hunt
... Most recent players to score on their first-team debut for Liverpool
1, Daniel Sturridge
2. Andre Wisdom
3. Luis Suarez

... Most recent players to score on their Premier League debut for Liverpool
1. Mohamed Salah
2. Sadio Mane
3. Victor Moses

... Seasons Liverpool won the Uefa Cup
1972–73, 1975–76 and 2000–01

Answers: 1960s Transfers

	Player	Signed from
1	Gordon Milne	Preston
2	Ian St John	Motherwell
3	Ron Yeats	Dundee United
4	Jim Furnell	Burnley
5	Geoff Strong	Arsenal
6	Emlyn Hughes	Blackpool
7	Ray Clemence	Scunthorpe
8	Alun Evans	Wolves
9	Alec Lindsay	Bury
10	Larry Lloyd	Bristol Rovers

Answers: Who Said That?

1. (b) Bill Shankly
2. (c) Gerard Houllier
3. (a) Bob Paisley
4. (b) Rafa Benitez
5. (b) Bill Shankly
6. (c) Kenny Dalglish (on how the S*n could make amends to Liverpool)
7. (c) Kevin Keegan
8. (a) Steven Gerrard
9. (b) Ray Clemence
10. (a) Bill Shankly

Answers: Name the season

1. 2009-10
2. 1986-87
3. 1971-72
4. 1989-90
5. 2015-16
6. 1991-92
7. 1995-96
8. 2001-02
9. 1981-82
10. 2017-18
11. 1977-78

Answers: Where are they from? (Part 2)

	Player	Country of birth
1	Alisson	Brazil
2	Adrian	Spain
3	Virgil van Dijk	Netherlands
4	Joël Matip	Cameroon
5	Fabinho	Brazil
6	Georginio Wijnaldum	Netherlands
7	Thiago	Spain
8	Naby Keïta	Guinea
9	Xherdan Shaqiri	Switzerland
10	Roberto Firmino	Brazil
11	Sadio Mane	Senegal
12	Mohamed Salah	Egypt
13	Diogo Jota	Portugal
14	Divock Origi	Belgium

Answers: Kevin Keegan

1. (c) Doncaster
2. (a) a brass works
3. (a) Scunthorpe
4. (b) £33,000
5. (a) £50 a week (Shankly had originally offered him £45)
6. (b) 323
7. (a) 100
8. (c) Johnny Giles
9. (b) He crashed his bicycle (despite suffering severe cuts Keegan secured second place in event, and won that edition of the show).
10. (a) 63
11. (c) Hamburg
12. (b) £500,000

13. (a) Head Over Heels in Love
14. (c) Southampton
15. (b) Brut

Answers: Shoot-outs - 1984 European Cup Final

1	Steve Nicol
2	Phil Neal
3	Graeme Souness
4	Ian Rush
5	Alan Kennedy

Answers: Who am I?

1. Joey Jones
2. Phil Neal
3. Phil Thompson
4. Ian Callaghan
5. Steve Heighway
6. David Fairclough
7. John Toshack
8. Steve McMahon
9. Jim Beglin
10. Alan Kennedy

Answers: Sadio Mane

1. (b) 1990
2. (a) Senegal
3. (c) Metz
4. (b) Red Bull Salzburg
5. (c) Southampton
6. (b) £11.8 million

7. (a) 2 mins 56 sec
8. (b) June 2016
9. (c) £34 million
10. (a) Liverpool Player of the Season
11. (c) Ethiad Stadium
12. (a) Porto
13. (c) 10
14. (b) 22
15. (c) 36

Answers: Club records

1. (b) 11–0 (v Strømsgodset in the European Cup Winners' Cup, 17 Sep 1974)
2. (a) 10–1 (v Rotherham in theSecond Division, 18 Feb 1899)
3. (b) 9-1 (v Birmingham in the Second Division, 11 Dec 1954)
4. (c) 32 (during the 2019–20 season)
5. (b) 101,254 (at the Michigan Stadium in Jul 2018 v Man United)
6. (b) 16 (in 42 games in the 1978–79 season).
7. (a) 18 (from 27 October 2019 to 24 Feb 2020)
8. (a) 9–0 (v Newtown in second qualifying round, 1889)
9. (b) 101 (in 2013–14)
10. (c) 85 (from 7 Feb 1978 to 31 Jan 1981).

Answers: Anfield

1. (b) Ireland
2. (a) 1884
3. (a) 5,000
4. (b) Archibald Leitch
5. (b) 61,905 (against Wolves in the 1951–52 FA Cup)

6. (b) 53,394
7. (c) 61,000
8. (b) £60 million
9. (c) 1906
10. (c) a hill in South Africa
11. (c) 30,000
12. (a) SS Great Eastern
13. (c) 1957
14. (b) The Shankly Gates
15. (b) 1992

Answers: Michael Owen

1. (a) Chester
2. (c) football
3. (c) 1996-97
4. (b) 17 yrs, 4mths (Owen scored on his debut, away at Wimbledon on 6 May 1997)
5. (a) £8 million
6. (b) 2001
7. (b) two (1997–98 & 1998–99)
8. (a) 40
9. (c) Argentina
10. (a) 1998
11. (a) 158
12. (b) 89
13. (b) Persil
14. (c) Newcastle
15. (b) Stoke City

Answers: Name the Five Players...

... Who have worn Liverpool's number five shirt in the Premier League

1. Mark Wright
2. Steve Staunton
3. Milan Baros
4. Daniel Agger
5. Georginio Wijnaldum

... Who have won the most England Caps while with Liverpool?
1. Steven Gerrard
2. Michael Owen
3. Emlyn Hughes
4. Ray Clemence
5. Jordan Henderson

... Who have scored the most goals for England with Liverpool?
1. Michael Owen
2. Steven Gerrard
3. Roger Hunt
4. Peter Crouch
5. Daniel Sturridge

... Who have appeared for both Liverpool & Everton in the Premier League?
David Burrows, Don Hutchinson, Nick Barmby, Abel Xavier and Sander Westerveld.
(In addition, Peter Beardsley and Gary Ablett played for Liverpool in Division One and Everton in the Premier League)

... Who have captained European Cup & Champions League winning teams
1 Emlyn Hughes
2 Phil Thompson
3 Graeme Souness

4 Steven Gerrard
5 Jordan Henderson

… To score UEFA Champions League hat-tricks with Liverpool
1. Michael Owen
2. Yossi Benayoun
3. Philippe Coutinho
4. Sadio Mane
5. Diogo Jota

Answers: How Tall? (Part 2)

	Player	Height
1	Ian Callaghan	5ft 7
2	Chris Lawler	6ft 0
3	Ian St John	5ft 7
4	Ron Yeats	6ft 2
5	Tommy Smith	5ft 10
6	Roger Hunt	5ft 9
7	Ray Clemence	6ft 0
8	Emlyn Hughes	5ft 11
9	Steve Heighway	5ft 10
10	John Toshack	6ft 1
11	Phil Thompson	6ft 0
12	Kevin Keegan	5ft 8
13	Jimmy Case	5ft 9
14	Terry McDermott	5ft 10
15	Ray Kennedy	5ft 11
16	Phil Neal	5ft 11
17	Joey Jones	5ft 11
18	David Fairclough	6ft 0
19	Sammy Lee	5ft 7
20	Kenny Dalglish	5ft 8

Answers: Shoot-outs - 2001 League Cup Final

1	Gary McAllister
2	Nick Barmby
3	Christian Ziege
4	Didi Hamann
5	Robbie Fowler
6	Jamie Carragher

Answers: The 1980–81 European Cup

1. (c) 10-1
2. (b) Souness & McDermott
3. (c) Aberdeen
4. (b) 5-0
5. (a) Graeme Souness
6. (c) CSKA Sofia
7. (a) Bayern Munich
8. (b) Ray Kennedy
9. (c) Parc des Princes.
10. (a) Real Madrid
11. (b) Alan Kennedy
12. (c) Souness & McDermott (who tied with Karl-Heinz Rummenigge on six goals)

Answers: Who Said That? (Part 2)

1. (b) Gerard Houllier
2. (c) Jurgen Klopp (on arriving at Liverpool in 2015)
3. (a) Bill Shankly
4. (a) Bob Paisley
5. (b) Steven Gerrard
6. (c) Kenny Dalglish
7. (b) Bill Shankly

8. (c) Rafa Benitez
9. (a) Bill Shankly
10. (b) Andy Robertson

Answers: 1970s Transfers

	Player	Signed from
1	Steve Heighway	Skelmersdale
2	John Toshack	Cardiff
3	Kevin Keegan	Scunthorpe
4	Peter Cormack	Notts Forest
5	Jimmy Case	South Liverpool
6	Alan Waddle	Halifax
7	Ray Kennedy	Arsenal
8	Phil Neal	Northampton
9	Terry McDermott	Newcastle
10	Joey Jones	Wrexham
11	David Johnson	Ipswich
12	Alan Hansen	Partick Thistle
13	Kenny Dalglish	Celtic
14	Steve Ogrizovic	Chesterfield
15	Graeme Souness	Middlesbrough
16	Kevin Sheedy	Hereford
17	Alan Kennedy	Newcastle
18	Frank McGarvey	St. Mirren
19	Avi Cohen	Maccabi Tel Aviv
20	Ronnie Whelan	Home Farm

Answers: Name the season 2

1. 2007-08
2. 1982-83
3. 1997-98
4. 1974-75
5. 1992-93
6. 1987-88
7. 2012-13
8. 1980-81
9. 2010-11
10.1990-91
11.1973-74

Answers: Robbie Fowler

1. (c) Toxteth
2. (b) 1993-94
3. (a) 4mins 33secs
4. (c) PFA Young Player of the Year:
5. (a) Liverpool dockers' strike
6. (b) knee
7. (b) one (in 2001)
8. (a) 26
9. (b) 171
10. (c) 330
11. (c) five (he became the fourth player in Liverpool's history to score five in a match)
12. (b) Leeds United
13. (c) £12 million
14. (c) Kevin Keegan (at Man City)
15. (a) Blackburn (in 2008)

Answers: Where are they from? (Part 3)

	Player	Country of birth
1	Avi Cohen	Israel
2	Craig Johnston	Australia
3	Bruce Grobbelaar	Zimbabwe
4	Jim Beglin	Rep of Ire
5	Jan Molby	Denmark
6	Glenn Hysen	Sweden
7	Ronny Rosenthal	Israel
8	Torben Piechnik	Denmark
9	Stig Inge Bjornebye	Norway
10	Phil Babb	Rep of Ire
11	Patrik Berger	Czech Rep
12	Karl-Heinz Riedle	Germany
13	Bjorn Tore Kvarme	Norway
14	Oyvind Leonhardsen	Norway
15	Brad Friedel	USA
16	Rigobert Song	Cameroon
17	Titi Camara	Guinea
18	Sander Westerveld	Netherlands
19	Vladimír Smicer	Czech Rep
20	Stephane Henchoz	Switzerland

Answers: Shoot-outs - 2005 Champ. League Final

1	Didi Hamann
2	Djibril Cisse
3	John Arne Riise
4	Vladimir Smicer

Answers: Jurgen Klopp

1. (a) Stuttgart
2. (b) 1967
3. (b) a doctor
4. (c) Mainz 05
5. (c) 6ft 4
6. (a) Mainz 05
7. (c) Borussia Dortmund
8. (b) two (2010–11, 2011–12)
9. (b) 2015
10. (c) Norbert
11. (a) Marko Grujic (who signed for £5.1m from Red Star Belgrade in January 2016).
12. (b) at an Oktoberfest
13. (c) Virgil Van Dijk (who signed from Southampton for £75m in January 2018)
14. (a) Opel
15. (c) Everton

Answers: Name the Six...

... Clubs that Liverpool beat in European Cup & Champions League finals
1 Borussia Mönchengladbach
2 Club Brugge
3 Real Madrid
4 AS Roma
5 AC Milan
6 Tottenham

... Liverpool players who have won BBC's Goal of the Season award
1. Terry McDermott
2. Ray Kennedy

3. John Aldridge
4. Dietmar Hamann
5. Steven Gerrard
6, Emre Can

… Players who've scored for Liverpool since January 2008 whose full names start and end with the same letter (e.g Robbie FowleR)
Soto Kyrgiakos, Andrea Dossena, Albert Riera, Nuri Sahin, Sebastian Coates and Alvaro Arbeloa.

Answers: Anagrams 2

1. Gary Gillespie
2. Jan Molby
3. Steve McManaman
4. Robbie Fowler
5. Michael Owen
6. Paul Ince
7. Steven Gerrard
8. James Milner
9. Sadio Mane
10. Andy Robertson

Answers: The 1983–84 European Cup

1. (a) Odense
2. (b) 6-0
3. (c) Bilbao
4. (a) Ian Rush
5. (b) Benfica
6. (c) Ronny Whelan
7. (b) Bucharest
8. (a) Ian Rush

9. (b) Stadio Olimpico
10. (b) 70,000
11. (c) Phil Neal
12. (a) Francesco Graziani

Answers: Emlyn Hughes

1. (a) Barrow-in-Furness
2. (c) rugby league
3. (a) Blackpool
4. (b) £65,000
5. (b) 665
6. (c) 49
7. (b) Crazy Horse (earned after he rugby-tackled Newcastle winger Albert Bennett)
8. (c) 62
9. (a) none (he was an unused squad member in 1970, and England failed to qualify in 1974 and 1978)
10. (c) four (1972–73, 1975–76, 1976–77, 1978–79)
11. (a) Wolves
12. (c) Gareth Edwards
13. (c) Swansea City
14. (a) Rotherham
15. (b) OBE

Answers: Shoot-outs - 2006 FA Cup Final

1	Didi Hamann
2	Sami Hyypia
3	Steven Gerrard
4	John Arne Riise

Answers: 1980s transfers

	Player	Signed from
1	Ian Rush	Chester
2	Bruce Grobbelaar	Vancouver Whitecaps
3	Craig Johnston	Middlesbrough
4	Mark Lawrenson	Brighton
5	Steve Nicol	Ayr United
6	Jim Beglin	Shamrock Rovers
7	Gary Gillespie	Coventry
8	Michael Robinson	Brighton
9	John Wark	Ipswich Town
10	Paul Walsh	Luton Town
11	Jan Molby	Ajax
12	Steve McMahon	Aston Villa
13	Barry Venison	Sunderland
14	John Aldridge	Oxford
15	Nigel Spackman	Chelsea
16	John Barnes	Watford
17	Peter Beardsley	Newcastle
18	Ray Houghton	Oxford
19	David Burrows	West Brom
20	Glenn Hysen	Fiorentina

	Player	Went to
1	Emlyn Hughes	Wolves
2	Steve Heighway	Minnesota Kicks
3	Ray Clemence	Tottenham
4	Jimmy Case	Brighton
5	Avi Cohen	Maccabi Tel Aviv
6	Ray Kennedy	Swansea
7	Richard Money	Luton
8	David Johnson	Everton

9	Terry McDermott	Newcastle
10	David Fairclough	Lucerne
11	Graeme Souness	Sampdoria
12	Michael Robinson	QPR
13	Phil Thompson	Sheffield United
14	Alan Kennedy	Sunderland
15	Phil Neal	Bolton
16	Sammy Lee	QPR
17	Ian Rush	Juventus
18	Paul Walsh	Tottenham
19	Nigel Spackman	QPR
20	John Aldridge	Real Sociedad

Answers: Who am I? (part2)

1. Mark Kennedy
2. John Scales
3. Glen Johnson
4. Fernando Torres
5. Jan Molby
6. John Aldridge
7. Divock Origi
8. Jordan Henderson
9. Craig Bellamy
10. John Arne Riise

Answers: Name the season 3

1. 1998–99
2. 2003-04
3. 2016-17
4. 1972-73
5. 2006-07

6. 1978-79
7. 1994-95
8. 2004-05
9. 1999–2000
10. 2011-12
11. 2005-06

Answers: Bill Shankly

1. (b) 1913
2. (c) Glenbuck, Ayrshire
3. (a) Miner
4. (c) four
5. (a) Preston North End
6. (b) Right-half
7. (a) £5 a week
8. (c) Air Force
9. (b) Carlisle United
10. (a) Huddersfield Town
11. (b) 1959
12. (c) three
13. (b) two
14. (a) Uefa Cup (1973)
15. (c) FA Cup final (1974)

Answers: Name the Seven...

... Brazilians who have played for Liverpool in the Premier League
Alisson, Fábio Aurélio, Philippe Coutinho, Doni, Fabinho, Roberto Firminoand Lucas Leiva.

... Germans who have played for Liverpool in the Premier League
Markus Babbel, Emre Can, Sean Dundee, Dietmar Hamann, Loris Karius, Karl-Heinz Riedle and Christian Ziege.

... Players who have played for Liverpool in the Premier League whose surname end in a double letter
Andy Carroll, Phil Babb, Steve Harkness, Dietmar Hamann, Jamie Redknapp, Sean Dundee and Harry Kewell

... Seasons when Liverpool won the FA Cup
1964–65, 1973–74, 1985–86, 1988–89, 1991–92, 2000–01 and 2005–06

Answers: How Tall? (Part 3)

	Player	Height
1	Alan Hansen	6ft 2
2	Alan Kennedy	5ft 10
3	Graeme Souness	5ft 11
4	Ronnie Whelan	5ft 9
5	Ian Rush	5ft 11
6	Bruce Grobbelaar	6ft 1
7	Mark Lawrenson	6ft 0
8	Steve Nicol	5ft 10
9	Craig Johnston	5ft 11
10	Gary Gillespie	6ft 2
11	Jan Molby	6ft 2
12	Ray Houghton	5ft 7
13	David Burrows	5ft 10
14	Steve McManaman	6ft 0
15	Rob Jones	5ft 8
16	Mark Wright	6ft 2

17	Michael Thomas	5ft 10
18	Robbie Fowler	5ft 9
19	Patrik Berger	6ft 1
20	Jamie Carragher	6ft 1

Answers: Shoot-outs - 2007 Champions Lge Semi

1	Bolo Zenden
2	Xabi Alonso
3	Steven Gerrard
4	Dirk Kuyt

Answers: 1990s transfers

	Player	Signed from
1	Jamie Redknapp	Bournemouth
2	Dean Saunders	Derby
3	Mark Walters	Rangers
4	Rob Jones	Crewe
5	Michael Thomas	Arsenal
6	David James	Watford
7	Stig Inge Bjornebye	Rosenborg
8	Nigel Clough	Notts Forest
9	Neil Ruddock	Tottenham
10	Phil Babb	Coventry
11	John Scales	Wimbledon
12	Mark Kennedy	Millwall
13	Stan Collymore	Notts Forest
14	Jason McAteer	Bolton
15	Karl-Heinz Riedle	Borussia Dortmund
16	Brad Friedel	Columbus Crew

17	Sami Hyypia	Willem II
18	Titi Camara	Marseille
19	Sander Westerveld	Vitesse Arnhem
20	Didi Hamann	Newcastle

	Player	Went to
1	Steve Staunton	Aston Villa
2	Gary Gillespie	Celtic
3	David Speedie	Blackburn
4	Steve McMahon	Man City
5	Gary Ablett	Everton
6	Barry Venison	Newcastle
7	Ray Houghton	Aston Villa
8	Steve Nicol	Notts County
9	Mark Walters	Southampton
10	Nigel Clough	Man City
11	Jan Molby	Swansea
12	John Scales	Tottenham
13	Stan Collymore	Aston Villa
14	John Barnes	Newcastle
15	Mark Kennedy	Wimbledon
16	Neil Ruddock	West Ham
17	Jason McAteer	Blackburn
18	David James	Aston Villa
19	Steve McManaman	Real Madrid
20	Bjorn Tore Kvarme	Saint-Etienne

Answers: The 2004-05 Champions League

1. (b) Grazer AK
2. (c) Olympiacos
3. (a) Monaco

4. (a) Luis García
5. (c) Bayer Leverkusen
6. (c) 6-2
7. (b) Sami Hyypia
8. (a) Juventus
9. (a) 0-0
10. (a) Luis García
11. (b) 4mins
12. (c) 6mins
13. (c) Atatürk Olimpiyat Stadı
14. (b) 72,059
15. (a) Paolo Maldini
16. (a) 1min
17. (b) Vladimir Smicer
18. (a) 60mins
19. (c) Dietmar Hamann
20. (b) Andriy Shevchenko

Answers: Who Said That? (Part 3)

1. (a) Gerard Houllier
2. (c) Jurgen Klopp
3. (a) Bill Shankly
4. (b) Kenny Dalglish
5. (b) Roy Evans
6. (c) Bill Shankly
7. (a) Emlyn Hughes
8. (c) Bob Paisley
9. (c) Alvaro Arbeloa
10. (b) Kevin Keegan

Answers: Alan Hansen

1. (a) Denmark (where his grandfather came from)
2. (c) he ran into a plate-glass panel
3. (b) golf
4. (a) Partick Thistle
5. (a) £110,000.
6. (c) 620
7. (b) Jockey
8. (b) 14
9. (c) eight (1978–79, 1979–80, 1981–82, 1982–83, 1983–84, 1985–86, 1987–88, 1989–90)
10. (a) 26
11. (b) 1985
12. (b) 6ft 2
13. (c) three
14. (c) 22 (1992 to 2014)
15. (a) Tall, Dark and Hansen

Answers: Name the Eight...

... Liverpool players to be named PFA Player of the Season
1. Terry McDermott
2. Kenny Daglish
3. Ian Rush
4. John Barnes
5. Steven Gerrard
6. Luis Suarez
7. Mohamed Salah
8. Virgil van Dijk

... Seasons when Liverpool won the League Cup
1980–81, 1981–82, 1982–83, 1983–84, 1994–95, 2000–01, 2002–03 and 2011–12

Answers: Where are they from? (Part 4)

	Player	Country of birth
1	Djimi Traore	Rep of Mali
2	Dietmar Hamann	Germany
3	Sami Hyypia	Finland
4	Christian Ziege	Germany
5	Markus Babbel	Germany
6	Jari Litmanen	Finland
7	Nicolas Anelka	France
8	Florent Pongolle	France
9	John Arne Riise	Norway
10	Jerzy Dudek	Poland
11	El Hadji Diouf	Senegal
12	Milan Baros	Czech Rep
13	Harry Kewell	Australia
14	Luis García	Spain
15	Djibril Cisse	France
16	Xabi Alons	Spain
17	Mohamed Sissoko	Rep of Mali
18	Fernando Morientes	Spain
19	Pepe Reina	Spain
20	Dirk Kuyt	Netherlands

Answers: Shoot-outs- 2012 League Cup Final

1	Steven Gerrard
2	Charlie Adam
3	Dirk Kuyt
4	Stewart Downing
5	Glen Johnson

Answers: 2000s transfers

	Player	Signed from
1	Emile Heskey	Leicester
2	Christian Ziege	Middlesbrough
3	John Arne Riise	Monaco
4	Milan Baros	Banik Ostrava
5	Chris Kirkland	Coventry
6	El Hadji Diouf	Lens
7	Harry Kewell	Leeds
8	Djibril Cisse	Auxerre
9	Xabi Alonso	Real Sociedad
10	Luis Garcia	Barcelona
11	Pepe Reina	Villarreal
12	Momo Sissoko	Valencia
13	Peter Crouch	Southampton
14	Daniel Agger	Brondby
15	Craig Bellamy	Blackburn
16	Dirk Kuyt	Feyenoord
17	Fernando Torres	Atletico Madrid
18	Martin Skrtel	Zenit St Petersburg
19	David N'Gog	Paris St Germain
20	Glen Johnson	Portsmouth

	Player	Went to
1	Stig Inge Bjornebye	Blackburn
2	Steve Staunton	Aston Villa
3	Robbie Fowler	Leeds
4	Sander Westerveld	Real Sociedad
5	Jamie Redknapp	Tottenham
6	Emile Heskey	Birmingham
7	Danny Murphy	Charlton
8	Michael Owen	Real Madrid

9	Vladimir Smicer	Bordeaux
10	El Hadji Diouf	Bolton
11	Milan Baros	Aston Villa
12	Didi Hamann	Bolton
13	Djimi Traore	Charlton
14	Luis Garcia	Atletico Madrid
15	Djibril Cisse	Marseille
16	Craig Bellamy	West Ham
17	Momo Sissoko	Juventus
18	Peter Crouch	Portsmouth
19	Steve Finnan	Espanyol
20	Robbie Keane	Tottenham

Answers: Steven Gerrard

1. (b) 1980
2. (a) 1998-99 (in a League match against Blackburn on 29 November 1998)
3. (b) 30
4. (c) 2005
5. (b) two (2000–01, 2005–06)
6. (c) Sami Hyypia
7. (c) 473
8. (c) 6ft
9. (b) four
10. (a) 54th
11. (b) Chelsea
12. (c) 710
13. (b) 186
14. (c) 114
15. (a) LA Galaxy

Answers: Who wins at Scrabble?

Highest
1. Alex Oxlade-Chamberlain
   (1,1,1,8,1,8,1,1,2,1,3,4,1,3,3,1,1,1,1,1,1)
2. Xherdan Shaqiri
   (8,4,1,1,2,1,1,1,4,1,10,1,1,1)
3. Georginio Wijnaldum
   (2,1,1,1,2,1,1,1,1,4,1,8,1,1,1,2,1,3)
4. Virgil van Dijk
   (4,1,1,2,1,1,4,1,1,2,1,8,5)
5. Trent Alexander-Arnold
   (1,1,1,1,1,1,1,1,8,1,1,2,1,1,1,1,1,1,1,2)

Lowest
1. Adrian
   (1,2,1,1,1,1)
2. Alisson
   (1,1,1,1,1,1,1,1)
3. Thiago
   (1,4,1,1,2,1)
4. Sadio Mane
   (1,1,2,1,1,3,1,1,1)
5. Fabinho
   (4,1,3,1,1,4,1)

Answers: Anfield Quiz 2

1. (a) 1963
2. (b) £350,000
3. (c) 6,700
4. (c) 1973
5. (b) 1994
6. (a) 12,390
7. (b) 1997

8. (a) He Made The People Happy
9. (c) 2017
10. (b) Bob Paisley
11. (b) 44,200
12. (c) 1.8 million
13. (b) £110million
14. (c) 20,676
15. (a) 80

Answers: The 2018-19 Champions League

1. (b) Daniel Sturridge
2. (a) 2nd
3. (c) Red Star Belgrade
4. (c) Mohamed Salah
5. (b) Napoli
6. (a) Paris Saint-Germain
7. (a) Joel Matip
8. (b) 3-1
9. (c) Porto
10. (a) Naby Keita
11. (c) Sadio Mané
12. (c) 6-1
13. (b) two
14. (a) Divock Origi
15. (c) Trent Alexander-Arnold
16. (b) 79mins
17. (c) Metropolitano Stadium
18. (b) Moussa Sissoko
19. (a) 22secs
20. (c) Divock Origi

Answers: Bob Paisley

1. (c) Durham
2. (b) 1919
3. (c) Bishop Auckland
4. (a) Army
5. (b) 1939
6. (c) 253
7. (a) Left-half
8. (a) three (1951-54)
9. (c) physiotherapist
10. (b) 1974
11. (c) six
12. (a) none
13. (c) six
14. (b) three
15. (b) OBE

Answers: Name the Ten...

...Goalkeepers who have worn Liverpool's number one shirt in the Premier League
1. Bruce Grobbelaar
2. David James
3. Sander Westerveld
4. Jerzy Dudek
5. Diego Cavalieri
6. Brad Jones
7. Loris Karius
8. Alisson Becker
9. Adrian
10. Caoimhin Kelleher

Answers: How Tall? (Part 4)

	Player	Height
1	Michael Owen	5ft 8
2	Danny Murphy	5ft 9
3	Steven Gerrard	6ft 0
4	Stéphane Henchoz	6ft 2
5	Sami Hyypia	6ft 4
6	Dietmar Hamann	6ft 3
7	Vladimír Smicer	5ft 11
8	Djimi Traore	6ft 3
9	Markus Babbel	6ft 3
10	Gary McAllister	6ft 1
11	Emile Heskey	6ft 2
12	Jerzy Dudek	6ft 2
13	John Arne Riise	6ft 1
14	Milan Baros	6ft 0
15	Harry Kewell	5ft 11
16	Luis García	5ft 9
17	Xabi Alonso	6ft 0
18	Djibril Cissé	6ft 0
19	Pepe Reina	6ft 2
20	Daniel Agger	6ft 3

Answers: Kenny Dalglish

1. (c) 1951
2. (b) Rangers
3. (a) Celtic
4. (b) 502
5. (a) 169
6. (c) 1983
7. (c) 102
8. (a) 1985

9. (b) Newcastle United
10. (c) eight (1978–79, 1979–80, 1981–82, 1982–83, 1983–84, 1985–86, 1987–88, 1989–90)
11. (a) none
12. (c) 1994–95
13. (b) three (1978, 1981, 1984)
14. (a) One (v Bruges, 1978)
15. (c) Knight Bachelor

Answers: Shoot-outs - 2016 League Cup Semi

1	Adam Lallana
2	Emre Can
3	Christian Benteke
4	Roberto Firmino
5	James Milner
6	Lucas Leiva
7	Joe Allen

Answers: Name the season 4

1. 1993-94
2. 1985-86
3. 2000–01
4. 2013-14
5. 1970-71
6. 1996-97
7. 2008-09
8. 1983-84
9. 2014-15
10. 1979-80
11. 2002-03

Answers: 2010s transfers

	Player	Signed from
1	Maxi Rodriguez	Atletico Madrid
2	Luis Suarez	Ajax
3	Jordan Henderson	Sunderland
4	Charlie Adam	Blackpool
5	Jordon Ibe	Wycombe
6	Joe Allen	Swansea
7	Philippe Coutinho	Inter Milan
8	Mamadou Sakho	Paris St Germain
9	Emre Can	Bayer Leverkusen
10	Divock Origi	Lille
11	Joe Gomez	Charlton
12	Roberto Firmino	1899 Hoffenheim
13	Christian Benteke	Aston Villa
14	Sadio Mane	Southampton
15	Georginio Wijnaldum	Newcastle
16	Mohamed Salah	Roma
17	Andy Robertson	Hull
18	Virgil Van Dijk	Southampton
19	Naby Keita	Red Bull Leipzig
20	Alisson Becker	Roma

	Player	Went to
1	Javier Mascherano	Barcelona
2	Fernando Torres	Chelsea
3	David N'Gog	Bolton
4	Dirk Kuyt	Fenerbahce
5	Maxi Rodriguez	Newell's Old Boys
6	Craig Bellamy	Cardiff
7	Charlie Adam	Stoke
8	Jonjo Shelvey	Swansea

9	Stewart Downing	West Ham
10	Luis Suarez	Barcelona
11	Pepe Reina	Bayern Munich
12	Daniel Agger	Brondby
13	Fabio Borini	Sunderland
14	Martin Skrtel	Fenerbahce
15	Jordon Ibe	Bournemouth
16	Joe Allen	Stoke
17	Mamadou Sakho	Crystal Palace
18	Philippe Coutinho	Barcelona
19	Danny Ings	Southampton
20	Simon Mignolet	Club Brugge

Answers: Kevin Keegan 2

1. (a) back
2. (c) Newcastle
3. (c) two (1978 and 1979)
4. (c) 1981–82
5. (b) 1995–96
6. (b) Fulham
7. (a) Sugar Puffs
8. (c) Manchester City
9. (c) two (1973 and 1976)
10. (a) 1972
11. (b) two (1977 for Liverpool and 1980 for Hamburg)
12. (c) 5ft 8
13. (b) OBE
14. (a) Two (he got the first two goals in the 3-0 win v Newcastle in 1974)
15. (b) three (1972–73, 1975–76, 1976–77)

Answers: Who Said That? (Part 4)

1. (c) Bill Shankly
2. (a) Rafa Benitez
3. (c) Jurgen Klopp
4. (b) Kevin Keegan
5. (a) Tommy Smith
6. (c) Ian St John
7. (b) Bill Shankly
8. (a) Bill Shankly
9. (c) Xabi Alonso
10. (a) Bob Paisley

Answers: Anagrams – Liverpool Managers

1. Kenny Dalglish
2. Rafael Benítez
3. Graeme Souness
4. Bill Shankly
5. Brendan Rodgers
6. Roy Hodgson
7. Gérard Houllier
8. Roy Evans
9. Bob Paisley
10. George Kay

Answers: Shoot-outs - 2019 European Super Cup

1	Roberto Firmino
2	Fabinho Tavarez
3	Divock Origi
4	Trent Alexander-Arnold
5	Mohamed Salah

Answers: Graeme Souness

1. (a) Edinburgh
2. (b) 1953
3. (c) Tottenham
4. (b) Middlesbrough
5. (a) £350,000
6. (b) 358
7. (a) 56
8. (c) Boys from the Blackstuff
9. (b) Sampdoria
10. (b) £650,000.
11. (c) Rangers
12. (a) 1991
13. (c) Dean Saunders
14. (c) Bristol City
15. (b) five (1978–79, 1979–80, 1981–82, 1982–83, 1983–84)

Answers: Name the Eleven

… Liverpool players who started the 1984 European Cup final
1. Bruce Grobbelaar
2. Phil Neal
3. Alan Kennedy
4. Mark Lawrenson
5. Ronnie Whelan
6. Alan Hansen
7. Kenny Dalglish
8. Sammy Lee
9. Ian Rush
10. Craig Johnston
11. Graeme Souness

... Liverpool players who started the 2005 Champions League Final

1. Jerzy Dudek
3. Steve Finnan
23. Jamie Carragher
4. Sami Hyypia
21. Djimi Traore
14. Xabi Alonso
10. Luis García
8. Steven Gerrard
6. John Arne Riise
7. Harry Kewell
5. Milan Baros

... Liverpool players who started the 2019 Champions League Final

13. Alisson
66. Trent Alexander-Arnold
32. Joël Matip
4. Virgil van Dijk
26. Andrew Robertson
14. Jordan Henderson
3. Fabinho
5. Georginio Wijnaldum
11. Mohamed Salah
9. Roberto Firmino
10. Sadio Mane

Answers: Past players (part 3)

	Player	Country of birth
1	Daniel Agger	Denmark
2	Javier Mascherano	Argentina
3	Yossi Benayoun	Israel
4	Ryan Babel	Netherlands

5	Fernando Torres	Spain
6	Lucas Leiva	Brazil
7	Albert Riera	Spain
8	David N'Gog	France
9	Martin Skrtel	Slovakia
10	Maxi Rodríguez	Argentina
11	Brad Jones	Australia
12	Luis Suarez	Uruguay
13	José Enrique	Spain
14	Fabio Borini	Italy
15	Kolo Toure	Senegal
16	Mamadou Sakho	France
17	Philippe Coutinho	Brazil
18	Simon Mignolet	Belgium
19	Emre Can	Germany
20	Christian Benteke	Belgium

Answers: Quiz That's Lacking in Options

1. John Toshack
2. 1965-66
3. Heskey
4. Southampton
5. Fratton Park and Filbert Street
6. David Speedie
7. Phil Chisnall (after signing for £25,000 in April 1964, the 21-year-old forward only managed two goals in eight appearances before moving to Southend in 1967)
8. Blackpool (Liverpool lost both their Premier League matches to them)
9. Ayresome Park
10. Rafael Benitez

How did you do?

	Max Score	Your Score
The Early Years	20	
Jamie Carragher	15	
The 1976-77 European Cup	12	
How Tall?	20	
Anagrams	10	
The Shoot-outs	6	
Mohamed Salah	15	
The 1977-78 European Cup	12	
Ian Rush	15	
Name the 3	12	
Transfers: The 1960s	10	
Who said that?	10	
Name the season	11	
Where are they from?	14	
Kevin Keegan	15	
Shoot-outs 2	5	
Who am I?	10	
Sadio Mane	15	
Club Records	10	
Anfield	15	
Michael Owen	15	
Name the 5	30	
How Tall? Past players	20	
Shoot-outs 3	6	
The 1980-81 European Cup	12	
Who said that? (part 2)	10	
Transfers: The 1970s	20	
Name the season (part 2)	11	
Robbie Fowler	15	
Where are they from? (part 2)	20	
Shoot-outs 4	4	
Jurgen Klopp	15	
Name the 6	18	
Anagrams 2	10	

The 1983-84 European Cup	12	
Emlyn Hughes	15	
Shoot-outs 5	4	
Transfers: The 1980s	40	
Who am I? (part two)	10	
Name the season (part 3)	11	
Bill Shankly	15	
Name the 7	28	
How Tall? (part 3)	20	
Shoot-outs 6	4	
Transfers: The 1990s	40	
The 2004-05 Champions League	20	
Who said that? (part 3)	10	
Alan Hansen	15	
Name the 8	16	
Where are they from? (part 3)	20	
Shoot-outs 7	5	
Transfers: The 2000s	40	
Steven Gerrard	15	
Who Wins at Scrabble?	10	
Anfield 2	15	
The 2018-19 Champions League	20	
Bob Paisley	15	
Name the 10	10	
How Tall? (part 4)	20	
Kenny Dalglish	15	
Shoot-outs 8	7	
Name the season (part 4)	11	
Transfers: The 2010s	40	
Kevin Keegan 2	15	
Who said that? (part 4)	10	
Anagrams Liverpool Managers	10	
Shoot-outs 9	5	
Graeme Souness	15	
Name the 11	33	
Where are they from? (part 4)	20	
A Quiz That's Lacking in Options	10	
Your Total		

Final Score

850 to 1,001
You're a Liverpool Legend—the King of the Kop.

700 to 849
Impressive. You're the stuff that Premier League winners are made of.

550 to 699
Congratulations—you're a First Team regular.

400 to 549
Your hard work has not gone unnoticed. You've earned a League debut.

250 to 399
Showing promise. You're on the bench for the League Cup games.

under 250
Report for double training.

If you enjoyed this book it would be great if you could give it a rating, or leave a review, on Amazon.

Ratings and reviews make the book more visible, which helps improve sales.

And I'm kinda broke right now.

Thanks,

Martin.

Printed in Great Britain
by Amazon

78769357R00119